CONTENTS

A Rough Guide to the Scottish Juniors

For starters let's kick off with the term "Junior football" which conjures up an image of young kids playing competitive matches, with irate parents arguing with each other before nearly exchanging blows on the touchline. This is of course schoolboy football, which is the first step before Youth(Under-19) and Juvenile(Under-21) level.

The Junior term isn't age related at all, it's a grade set up by the Scottish Football Association. The Senior grade refers to the top four leagues from the Scottish Premier League to the Scottish Football League, as well as the four Senior non-leagues - the Highland Football League, Lowland Football League, East of Scotland Football League and the South of Scotland Football League.

The Scottish Junior FA was formed in October 1886, although Junior football had been played since around 1880 in local associations throughout the country. The SFA united the Junior clubs under one association and established the Scottish Junior Cup as a national competition with 39 clubs taking part in the 1886-87 season. The first winners of the trophy were Govan based Fairfield who beat Edinburgh Woodburn 3-1 in the inaugural final.

The SJFA established major reforms in 1968, with the first phase of regionalisation replacing many local associations with six regional committees - Ayrshire, Central, East, Fife, Tayside and North. Then in 2002 the last major reformation as the six regions were split into three larger regional sections of North, East and West.

From the 2007-08 season the Superleague winners of the three regions as well as the Scottish Junior Cup winners automatically qualified for the first round of the following season's Scottish Cup, so the Junior clubs could now pit their wits against the Senior sides. From 2007, Givan, followed by Banks O' Dee and Linlithgow Rose in 2014, qualify for the Scottish Cup every season as they are also full members of the SFA.

As from the start of the 2016-17 season there are 159 members of the SJFA - North Region (35 clubs) East Region (60 clubs) West Region (64 clubs) with each region contains several divisions, the East and West regions also being split into further geographical sections in the lower divisions. All members club take part in the Scottish Junior Cup when is affectionately known as the "Holy Grail" of Junior football. In 1922 -23 an astounding 412 clubs set out on the long trail for glory when a crowd of around 20,000 witnessed Musselburgh Bruntonians beat Arniston Rangers 3-0 in an all-East final at Tynecastle.

Hampden Park regularly hosted the final until 1986, where a record attendance was set in 1951 when Petershill beat Irvine Meadow in front of 77,650 spectators, followed by 69,959 at the Kilbirnie Ladeside v Camelon final the following year. Nowadays the final is played at a geographical neutral senior league ground with Rugby Park in Kilmarnock being a regular venue in recent years.

The clubs compete in a straight knockout competition for the Junior Cup with no regional draws or seeds, only first round byes for the three regional champions, cup holders and the aforementioned three SFA member clubs.

On the Trail of the Scottish Holy Grail

Shaun E Smith

DEDICATION

Timothy James Paul Peter Smith

Gone from us too soon.

Thank you for guiding me on my way.

I hope I've made you proud.

1. THE CONCEPT

(December 2014)

I've always suffered from some form of obsessive compulsive disorder, even before OCD was something I was fully aware of. I suppose the blame originates back to my childhood when I spent my pocket money on Soccer Star cards and Merlin sticker albums, with the "Got, not got, got" culture being my first obsession of collecting things and desperately attempted to complete a full set. Also, there was football programmes to collect, making sure I secured a copy of every Newcastle United home issue. Inside each programme was a token, which you cut out and glued onto a sheet, which was used as a way of purchasing a match ticket, in the unlikely event of the lads getting to a cup final at Wembley. So even way back then I was deluded to think we were going to actually win something.

Apart from football my other passion is my incredibly good taste in music. As a teenager, my love of bands like The Jam, Stiff Little Fingers and The Clash meant I had to possess their complete discography in my vinyl collection. Even now in my middle age years, I have everything by my favourite artists, be it every album and single by Teenage Fanclub, the complete works of Half Man Half Biscuit or all 31 studio albums by The Fall.

Okay, this isn't exactly an anxiety disorder leading to repetitive behaviour or serious compulsions. I'm also aware that OCD is serious so I don't mean to trivialize it by comparing it to collecting records, pin badges, scarves, mugs and any old tat which bears the name Newcastle United FC.

My football ground obsession began when I regularly followed the Magpies away from home in the early 1980's. The list of grounds snowballed, with the possibility of maybe doing all 92 grounds in (as it was then) the Football League. As it later materialized it became more difficult to see my team play at new grounds, having to rely on cup draws or the odd pre-season friendly or testimonial. For various reasons and with a heavy heart I cancelled my season ticket at St James Park in 2009, upon which I decided to go all out in completing "The 92" After a few seasons travelling to all corners of England and Wales I finally achieved my goal in November 2011 at the Amex Stadium, which was the brand-new home of Brighton & Hove Albion.

Since then my Groundhopping activities has involved chipping away at the Scottish 42, completing the Conference, going to organised groundhops and having days out in towns and cities which have plenty of decent pubs and a good ground to visit. As much as I've enjoyed this random ground bagging over the last few years there's been something lacking, the need to chase a total and an obsession to complete another set. I could have easily attempted to complete another league, but I wanted to do something slightly different and above all something enjoyable and not extremely difficult.

In November 2014 I was preparing for another trip to Edinburgh, picking out a visit to Tranent Juniors in the East Region South Division. As part of the My Matchday reports on my blog I include a potted history of the club, so as I researched their past I discovered they were yet another club which had won the prestigious Scottish Junior Cup. This was the moment when a cloud appeared over my head filled with a light bulb and the birth of an incredible idea.

I immediately researched the history of the Holy Grail of Scottish Junior football, discovering that since the competition began in 1886-87 there have been 66 clubs which have lifted the top prize. Out of those previous winners there are 14 clubs that no longer exist and I've ticked off 8 of those remaining clubs already, so that makes it a grand total of 44 former cup winners to visit. Now this wouldn't generally be too much of a problem but there's two major factors blocking my path; firstly, my job requires me to work on Saturday mornings with just one full weekend off once a month and secondly, I don't live in Scotland; residing 60 miles south of the border, born and bred in between a huge monument of an angel and a river which is crossed by seven bridges.

So, to make this task more feasible I really need to narrow down the odds a bit. In my lifetime, which hits the half a century in 2015 there's been 28 Junior Cup winners, with only one club no longer around and five clubs I've already been to before, which leaves a more practicable total of 22 trophy winners since the 1965-66 season.

After my visit to Tranent, who are a club which lifted the trophy 30 years before I was born, I declared on my blog that I willing to accept this challenge, not only for visiting 22 grounds in different parts of Scotland, but so I can hopefully also fulfil an ambition of writing a book about my Groundhopping exploits in celebration of my 50th birthday.

I don't know how long this pursuit will take or what fate has in store, so as I write this chapter a few days before

Christmas 2014, I don't know if this latest obsession will eventually be achieved. If you're reading this publication and haven't cheated and went straight to the last chapter or just casually flicking through it then I must have overcome the crisis of reaching "the big five O" by achieved my target of completing another set.

2 HIGH TIDE LOW TIDE

Largs Thistle - Barrfield Stadium (August 2008)

Before this escapade gets underway, I need to start before the beginning with my first visit to a Scottish Junior ground. In 2008 finances dictated there was no luxurious family holiday abroad, which meant swapping hot sunny beaches, cold San Miguel and a guaranteed bronzed tan in exchange for damp cold weather, warm beer, karaoke and bingo. I booked two caravan holidays exploring the west coast of Britain, made up of a week in north-west Wales followed by a trip north of the border to Wemyss Bay in Inverclyde, on the beautiful Firth of Clyde.

As is always the case while on vacation, both holidays had to include taking in a local football match. The previous week I was at Prestatyn Town and there were several ground bagging options available in week two. The Scottish season had just got under way the previous weekend, but I really fancied visiting a Junior ground after Jamie Wire's excellent website Non-League Scotland had stirred my interest.

Upon checking the fixtures, I found that Largs Thistle were playing their opening home game of the season, in the Ardagh Glass League Cup against Kilwinning Rangers, just a short 15-minute drive from the caravan park, with a convenient early evening kick-off time of 7 o'clock.

The day prior to the game we drove down to Largs, and found it a quite tranquil little town, even though it's now geared towards tourists. It's the sort of place where you would retire to after living in Glasgow through your working life, in a similar way that I would like to spend my own retirement in Tynemouth or better still in Alnmouth, although a lottery win or a beneficiary from an unknown rich relative is the only way this dream could possibly become a reality.

The town has a Victorian promenade and lies close to the Isle of Cumbrae, which is just a mile offshore with regular ferry services across to the island. The name translates from Scottish Gaelic as 'the slopes', with historical connections with the Vikings. The Battle of Largs in 1263 saw the Scots attack Norwegians bidding to salvage ships from the army fleet of King Magnus III. The town is home to the award winning Vikingar Centre in Barrfields, not far from the football ground. The battle is commemorated with an annual Viking festival held in the town, which includes battle re-enactments and climaxes in a grand Viking burning and fireworks display.

While in the town I checked the whereabouts of Barrfield Park in preparation for the following night, which I found easily enough on Brisbane Road, with the interior of the ground clearly visible through the aluminium fence. The ground has an oval appearance with terracing curling around three sides, and dominated by the barrel roofed main stand on the far side. Largs have played at Barrfield since it opened in July 1930 and the ground's current capacity is 4,500 with 800 bench seats.

The 'Theestle' formed in 1920, however there was an original Largs Thistle formed in 1889. Although the current club has little connection to the original, the earlier date is still officially recognised, after the SJFA produced a centenary book in 1986 stating this fact. Largs won promotion to the Scottish Football Junior West Division One, after winning the Ayrshire District League in 2004/05, but more importantly for this book, they are previous winners of the Scottish Junior Cup.

On the 15th May 1994, they reached the final against Glenafton Athletic as unfancied underdogs in front of 8,000 spectators at Ibrox Stadium. In a match, which the local press labelled a 'David vs Goliath' contest, it was Davy who triumphed winning 1-0 with Pat McCurdy grabbing the decisive goal.

The week which lead to the club winning the biggest prize in Scottish Junior football was also a quite significant time in my own life and a personal turning point. The previous weekend Newcastle hosted Arsenal for the last game in our first season in the new Premier League. This was exactly like the old Football League Division One, but with referees wearing green shirts and a satellite TV channel throwing their weight behind it with piles of cash. United won 2-0 on that afternoon, with a brace from Andy Cole which rounded off a fantastic campaign. The third-place finish booked a return to European football for the first time since 1977, so I was thrilled at the prospect of doing some grounds abroad. After the match, me and my mate Zippy and a few pals from work stayed out and celebrated in the Bigg Market late into the night, but if that was marvellous, then there isn't a superlative big enough to describe what happened the following evening. The best-looking lass in Low Fell who I desperately wanted to go out with, agreed to go on a date with me. Akin to Largs Thistle, I spent the whole of that week excited but nervous for the big day. As first dates go it turned out to be a classic and the rest as they say is history, as twenty years later me and "the breadknife" are still going strong.

I drove down from Wemyss Bay to Largs for the match alone, leaving Debra with our two children Laura and James at the caravan park. At the time the kids were still bairns, Laura was twelve and James ten years old in August 2008. Even at this young age they had already grown accustomed to their Dad knicking off to a match somewhere during the holidays.

After 24 hours of fabulous holiday weather of dull skies and constant rain, I feared a postponement until arriving to find the players on the pitch doing their pre-match warm ups and the pitch looking in excellent condition. I had contacted the club prior to heading off on holiday to make some general inquiries, so on arrival I was greeted with a warm welcome by club secretary Donald Reid, who invited me into the hospitality cabin for a cup of tea at half time. As I'm not one to knock back a freebie I took up Don's kind offer, where apart from a cuppa and a biscuit, I was also giving a club pennant as a souvenir of my visit, which still has pride of place at home alongside my autographed Newcastle United Fairs Cup winner's pennant and the first one produced by Gateshead FC in 1977.

The match kicked off with Largs dominated the first half creating several chances in the opening stages, until the visitors task was made much harder with the dismissal of Gavin Orr for an off the ball incident, which was spotted by the linesman. Moments later Largs took the lead when a pinpoint cross from the right was firmly headed home by James Marks. Just prior to halftime, another header, this time on the end of a corner kick from Neil Shearer, the biggest lad on the field (never thought I'd see another

Shearer goal again) who celebrated by yelling "Girrrin!" before being mobbed by his teammates.

Kilwinning slightly improved after half time. I walked past a few of their fans, who were giving the ref and linesman some serious abuse, obviously upset at the dismissal and every decision made thereafter. The weather deteriorated, with the swirling wind and rain somewhat spoiling the game.

Rangers managed to get back into it on 83 minutes when McGregor fired in a penalty, but this was merely a consolation as minutes later Marks got his second of the night, a fine run and cross from Craig Black was finished off with a neat flick at the near post to make it 3-1, which capped off an enjoyable game considering the poor conditions.

During the game, I did a rough head count of the attendance and estimated a crowd of around 160. I was later informed there were only 53 paying punters on the night, with a few arriving after the gateman left, plus a few young'uns (who congregate at the bottom end of the stand drinking cans of Tennent's lager) may have sneaked into the bottom end of the ground for free. At the time this was probably the lowest attendance between the two clubs when you compare it to the 6,151 who attended a semi-final between the two sides in the 1990's.

Since my visit to Largs the town has drawn my attention twice in recent years. In 2011 residents Colin and Chris Weir won £161,000,000 on a Euromillions, the largest lottery win in the UK to date. Then in 2014 Kurt Cobain's favourite band The Vaselines shot a music video on the seafront for their single 'High Tide Low Tide' but more importantly what about Largs Thistle and the goings on at Barrfield since 2008.

Well nine months after this game both teams went in different directions with Largs winning promotion to the Super League Premier Division, while their opponents that evening, Kilwinning Rangers were relegated to the Ayrshire District League. The club went on to reach the Scottish Junior Cup final for a second time in 2010, again playing the underdog role against Linlithgow Rose, however there was no giant killing feat on this occasion as they narrowly lost by a solitary goal at Rugby Park. The following season they finished 5th, their highest ever league placing before the yo-yo effect between the top two divisions in recent years. Barrfield Stadium now boasts a 3G pitch which makes it a good backup plan for Groundhoppers attending matches on the west coast, however I would highly recommend a priority visit as they're a smashing little club and personally an excellent baptism into the world of Scottish Junior football.

Matchday Stats

Wednesday 6th August 2008 (7pm ko)

Ardagh Glass League Cup (Section One)

Largs Thistle 3(Marks 33,86. Shearer 43)

Kilwinning Rangers 1(McGregor 83pen)

Att. 160.est

Ground no.180

3. OUT OF TOWN

Bo'ness United - Newtown Park (May 2011)

Camelon Juniors - Carmuirs Park (May 2014)

I started writing my groundhopping blog in 2006 and at the same time formed *The 100 Football Grounds Club*. The simple reason for starting a groundhopping club was to assemble a community of football fans who also endure the football fan ailment known as stadiumitis. This was well before social media took off, so to find fellow footy fans who share the same hobby as myself was difficult at first, but eventually the club snowballed to the point where I had to close membership.

This was the first time I had written anything (apart from the odd love note to Debra) since leaving school a quarter of a century earlier. As you may already be aware my writing technique won't win any literary awards, as it's more of a friendly arm around the shoulder type style, with no clever cloggs long words which will have you thumbing through the dictionary.

My initial aim with the club was to gather together a squad of groundhoppers which did eventually come to fruition, as I began to meet up with fellow enthusiasts in various parts of the country to attend matches at new grounds together.

For the final match of the 2009-10 season I rounded off my season by visiting my second Junior ground, keeping up my tradition of my final new ground being a Scottish tick. Since I've started writing the blog and bagging different football grounds I've got into the habit of finishing the season in Scotland. This is another of my strange idiosyncrasies, I don't know why, but I think of it as a good luck omen for the following season.

All football fans suffer from various traits and superstitions, with the most familiar habit being the wearing of a lucky scarf, shirt or the same pair of undercrackers. I've had a few classics over the years. In 1983 my mate "Jimmy Jimmy" was trying to lose weight, so on one Saturday before the pub and the match we called into the weigh house in the Grainger Market, which has those old fashioned big scales which give you an accurate reading to the precise ounce. On that afternoon, Newcastle hammered promotion rivals Manchester City 5-0 which included a Peter Beardsley hat-trick. Obviously, this majestic performance was all down to our visit to the weigh house, so this triggered us both getting weighed on matchday for the rest of the season. We won promotion in what was a terrific season, so it obviously worked!

At the turn of the century we qualified for the Champions League two seasons on the spin, as "The Entertainers" returned playing a brand of all out attacking football. It wasn't the Shearer-Bellamy partnership, the flair of Laurent Robert or the managerial expertise of Sir Bobby Robson which got us there, no, that was all down to me, walking the same route to the match from The Black Garter. Every home game I marched my pals through the Greenmarket in to Eldon Square, through Top Shop onto Gallowgate, then along to the ground passing The Strawberry pub.

I've took the train journey from Newcastle Central Station to Edinburgh numerous times over the last 10 years. On this occasion one of Groundhopping squad - Jamie McQueen was sitting in his car on Waverley Bridge ready to chauffer me down to Newtongrange Star for their East Region Super League fixture with Lochee United. Nitten, as it is locally known have won the Scottish Junior Cup, but that victory came 35 years before I was born, so a few decades too early to qualify for this particular publication.

My first meeting with Jamie was in Paisley in January 2008 to visit the splendid Love Street before St Mirren got the bulldozers in and we've remained good friends since. Although he lives in Edinburgh, he originally hails from Dumfries so is naturally a Queen of the South fan. However, the main football love of his life is Liverpool, having been a fan since childhood, attending his first match at Anfield in 1989 for his ninth birthday.

Jamie is the definition of being fitba daft! He travels down to Anfield for all the home games as well as most away matches, with the game at St James Park being his season favourite, not because of the usual three points but meeting with yours truly for a pre-match pub crawl around the Toon. When he's not watching the reds, he'll go to any game, attending a match almost every night of the week.

On our arrival at New Victoria Park it was a pleasant surprise to be greeted by a recent addition to my little Groundhoppers club - James Little, who had come to the match specially to meet me, which was a nice gesture, but little did I know at the time that this would be the first of many.

James also lives in Edinburgh with his football allegiance lying with the Jam Tarts. As far as Junior football is concerned his team is Penicuik Athletic, where at the club's old Eastfield Park ground he attended his very first match as an eight-year-old in 1964.

He is always good enough to offer a lift from Edinburgh to whatever match of my choosing, all he asks in return is that I buy him a pie at half time. When I announced my plans for this book, he quickly got in touch to tell me he was looking forward to doing some of the 22 grounds with me, so I imagine he's going to play a crucial part, especially with some of the trickier destinations.

Fast forward one year and my final match of the season on the corresponding Saturday. I met up with James to visit my third Junior ground for the big title six-pointer in the East Region Super League, probably the country's biggest game of the day apart from that small matter of the Scottish Cup final between Dundee United and Ross County taking place at Hampden Park.

The match in question was at Bo'ness United for the big local derby with Linlithgow Rose at the top of the East Region Super League. Borrowstounness, which is more commonly known as Bo'ness is a coastal town in the Central Lowlands on the south bank of the Firth of Forth, found six miles east of Falkirk.

Bo'ness is now chiefly a commuter town with residents travelling to work in Edinburgh, Glasgow and Falkirk, but historically a centre of heavy industry, coal mining and a major port, where the shipbreaking industry dates to the twelfth century. The town's full name is rarely used nowadays, the population of over 14,000 favouring the moniker of Bo'ness.

Bo'ness United formed in 1945 when former Scottish League club Bo'ness merged with the junior club Bo'ness

Cadora. The club joined the Edinburgh & District League, which they won three times in their early years as well as appearing in two Scottish Junior Cup finals. In only their second competitive season they were unbeaten in 35 matches until an injury plagued team lost the final to Shawfield, but they returned the following year to lift the famous old trophy with a 2-1 win over Irvine Meadow.

Two further league titles in the 1950s and 1960s, plus more success in the Junior Cup finally followed in 1975 when they hammered Darvel 3-0 in the final. Their next appearance in the season finale came in 1979 when they were a narrowly beating by Camelon and they again tasted defeat, this time losing the 1983 final 2-0 against East Kilbride Thistle. Bo'ness had now appeared in five Junior Cup finals and their two triumphs came in matches in which they wore a changed strip, instead of their usual blue shirts and white shorts. They returned the following season, in traditional apparel for the 1984 with Baillieston at Ibrox Park. The B.U.'s went into the final as underdogs but a brace from Lex Shields secured a 2-0 victory to bring the trophy back to Newtown Park, a feat which they haven't managed to achieve since.

The BU's were East Region Division 1 champions for a second time in 2007-08, winning promotion to the East Super League and were the current title holders when I visited in May 2011. That 2009-10 success was their first top division championship since 1969, leading the table from start to finish, clinching the title in a thrilling final league match against their feisty neighbours Linlithgow Rose.

The 16-mile drive from Edinburgh to Bo'ness and the return journey included a liquid stop at The Duddingston

Arms in Newton. We arrived at Newtown Park to find a healthy crowd gathering for the much-anticipated clash. For the second successive year, the two fierce rivals met with the title up for grabs, but this season it's both clubs challenging for the league, locked on the same points with the hosts having a superior goal difference.

Newtown Park has always been home to Bo'ness United, and used as a football ground since the 1880s. The ground has a capacity of 7,500 made up of terracing on three sides with one side of cover. The traditional old main Stand was no longer used by spectators as it's been declared derelict with only the changing rooms in use. The classic looking wooden structure had elevated seating with a standing paddock at the front with blue wooden supports and beams, but unfortunately since my visit the south side stand is no more. Opposite is the terrace enclosure which cost £80,000 and runs in length between the two 18 yard lines, which has a silver frame with the club name and crest on its fascia.

I must have caught Bo'ness on an off day because they didn't look like a team at the top of the table, maybe the recent hectic schedule had taken its toll as they were comprehensively beaten by their old enemy from three and a half miles down the road.

Linlithgow took the lead halfway through the first half when Nelson latched on to a deflected shot to fire home and they continued to press with some top class saves from the United keeper maintaining the slender score line at the interval.

Two minutes after the restart Tommy Coyne capitalised on a goalmouth scramble to double the lead and from then on they were never in danger of letting the lead slip. Herd latched on to a free kick to nod home on 63 minutes and McLennan capped off a fine performance with a fine effort from a tight angle five minutes from time to make it 4-0.

A Bo'ness victory would have seen them needing just a single point from their final two games to clinch the title, but this victory for Rose meant "the Bee-yoo", assuming Linlithgow win their final match against Bonnyrigg, need maximum points from their remaining fixtures.

So, the title race was still wide open but on the evidence of this display its Linlithgow Rose that looked championship material. Well that's what I wrote on my blog in my matchday report the following day, but what do I know? If I could predict football results, then I wouldn't need to work as I would just rake in the cash from winning football bets. The following weekend Bo'ness won away at Forfar 2-0 which wasn't a surprise, whilst at the same time Linlithgow lost 2-4 at home to Bonnyrigg in the Battle of the Roses, a match which my travel companion James attended, so alas Bo'ness had retained the East Region Super League.

The club went on to complete a hat-trick of championships in 2013-14 and in 2016 after a gap of 17 years they won the East of Scotland Junior Cup for a fifth time.

Historically the town has links to the Roman period and marks the eastern extent of the Antonine Wall which stretched 39 miles from Bo'ness to Old Kilpatrick on the west coast of Scotland. Known to the Romans as Vallum Antonini, it was a turf fortification on stone foundations across the Central Belt of Scotland, representing the northernmost frontier barrier of the Roman Empire.

Just under a mile south of the wall is Camelon, a large settlement in the Forth Valley, found just over a mile west of Falkirk town centre. Along this stretch of the Antonine Wall the first fort was built in this area between AD80 to AD83 during the campaigns of governor Gnaeus Julius Agricola. The fort was excavated in 1900 and between 1975 and 1979, when a variety of bronze artefacts dating back to AD86 were discovered.

After the Romans withdrew, the name of Camelon disappeared for nigh on fifteen hundred years until the prominence of Iron and the cutting of the Forth and Clyde Canal in the 18th century. The population of Camelon was about 600 at the start of the 19th century, with most of the townsfolk working in the nail making industry. The completion of the Union Canal in 1822 saw the town expand with new houses, workshops and Inns along the banks of Port Downie.

Nowadays the population is around 4,500, with the locks which joined the Union Canal with the Forth and Clyde Canal replaced by the Falkirk Wheel in 2002. The rotating boat lift is just 2 miles from Camelon and attracts around 400,000 tourists every year, me included, being one of the million plus customers to have taking a boat trip through the wheel.

As for the football club, Camelon Juniors formed in 1920 and were members of the Stirlingshire, Intermediate and Lothian Leagues before reorganisation, when they joined the East Region of the SJFA. The Mariners reached their first of three Scottish Junior Cup finals in 1952, when they were beaten 1-0 by Kilbirnie Ladeside, before eventually taking honours in the Fife & Lothians Cup in 1971, the

Browns Cup in 1977 and were East Region Division One winners in 1979-80.

Camelon enjoyed their most triumphant spell in the mid-1990s, winning the Scottish Junior Cup in 1995 with a 2-0 win over Whitburn and reached the final the following year, but lost out to Tayport after extra-time. During this era, their trophy haul included adding two further league titles, the East of Scotland Junior Cup and the Skol League Cup.

In 2005-06 they won they won a second Lothian District League Division One title in three years and completed a double in the Fife & Lothians Cup. The Mariners reached their highest ever position in the Scottish Junior set up in 2008-09 when finishing runners-up to Bonnyrigg Rose in the East Region Super League.

My appearance at Camelon was obviously for my last new ground of the season in May 2014. Being a regular visitor to Edinburgh over the last decade I've developed the same routine. My morning starts with a hearty breakfast at the Babylon Cafe on South Bridge, which is one of those good old fashioned greasy spoons with the bench seats and tables bolted to wall. If this isn't the best breakfast in Edinburgh for under a fiver, then it must be in the Top 2 as the fry up is always cooked to perfection. Once I've been fed I have a walk around the record shops, as I love buying vinyl, just like a woman loves buying shoes. This is something I inherited from my Dad, as I remember as a bairn going around second hand record shops with him, digging through vinyl and looking for bargain pieces of plastic.

I met up with James Little in the Standing Order pub at noon, as on this occasion we were catching the train. We caught the 1303 Dunblane Service to Camelon which is a train line I've got to know pretty well, as this is the fifth different station I've alighted for a game. The journey took around 35 minutes so we had time for a swift one in the Canal Inn before the 2.30pm kick off. At the game, it was good to meet someone from the Groundhopping club, as Chris Sanderson was covering the game for The Scottish Sun. Chris hails from Ashington but now lives in Paisley, reporting on matches in the Scottish Juniors as well as the Scottish League. His knowledge of Junior football means he could be a good contact during the composition of this book.

Camelon Juniors played their early days without a home of their own, having to play prestigious Scottish Cup "home" games at the likes of Bo'ness and Stirling. The club committee approached George Strang, a local farmer who had extensive land on the north side of the canal. The landowner was swayed into an agreement when he heard that two of the Camelon players had served in the army, giving the club use of a field on Carmuirs farm.

Carmuirs Park is a typical classic Scottish Juniors ground dominated by terracing, although there is one glaring error at the old turnstile entrance with the added apostrophe which shows you're at Camelon Junior's. The North Enclosure at the entrance side covers two-thirds of the pitch, while on the canal side there's a smaller enclosure, with the changing room block, team dugouts and a refreshment bar. Both stands are decked out in red with CJFC and the team crest on the facade. There's further terracing behind the goal and at the far end there's grass banking in front of the houses, where one bloke stood on a shed roof watching the watch with a gigantic umbrella. I didn't know if he was part of the staff or just a some tight get watching the match for nowt from his back garden.

This was the first weekend of glorious hot weather so trust me to head to the only part of the UK where it was lashing down. The match against Bonnyrigg Rose kicked off in a heavy downpour but the hosts made a bright start taking a 16th minute lead. The Rose defence failed to clear a Callum Scott cross and the ball fell nicely to Colin Allison to fire home from close range. The visitors levelled twenty minutes later when a lovely cross from McLeish was met by a superb header from Dean Whitson, before finished the half strongly, taking an injury time lead when a clearance from a corner kick was recycled back into the box for Chris Renton to score.

The Mariners levelled just after the hour mark when a lovely passage of build-up play was finished off by Stephenson, but they were outdone by a replica goal by Whitson, who again combined with McLeish with a firm header on 77 minutes. Camelon pushed for an equaliser but Bonnyrigg held firm to take the three points in an enjoyable game to finish of ground bagging season.

After the match, me and James legged it back to the train station for the 1628 back to Edinburgh. As we are both keen runners we easily made it in the allotted seven minutes from the full-time whistle, which gave us more drinking time at The Guildford, one of my favourite pubs in the city. It was a good choice as they had a mini festival of ales from the Big Wolf Brewery as well as a great selection of other beers. I caught the 7pm train a bit pie-eyed and slept all the way home after another excellent day, with a cracking ground, a decent game, a canny drink and even a gift. My companion for the day gave me his brand-new football jersey from the Scotland Supporters Club, which is like the shirts worn in the 1974 World Cup. But why would an Englishman want a Scotland shirt you may ask. Well turn the page to find out why and read about another two Junior grounds which will bring the Scottish Joins trail up to date, before this escapade gets underway.

Matchday Stats

Saturday 21st May 2011 (2pm ko)

East Region Super League

Bo'ness United 0

Linlithgow Rose 4(Nelson 22,Coyne 47, Herd 63, McLennan 85)

Att.700.est   Ground no.289

Saturday 17th May 2014 (2pm ko)

East Region Super League

Camelon Juniors 2(Allison 16 Stephenson 61)

Bonnyrigg Rose 3(Whitson 36,77 Renton 45+3)

Att.190.est   Ground no.398

4. Everything's Roses

Bonnyrigg Rose - New Dundas Park (May 2013)

Linlithgow Rose - Prestonfield (November 2013)

Although I was obviously unaware of it, the first football season in of my existence was in 1965-66. This was a campaign which saw Newcastle United finish 15th in the old First Division and suffer early exits from both cup competitions, so on that score nothing much has changed over the last 50 years.

I was born in a terraced flat, a stone's throw from the River Tyne in the Teams area of Gateshead, but by the time this season concluded my mam and dad moving us to our first proper family home with an inside toilet! Also around this time there was a World Cup tournament taking place, which was won by the host nation who played all six games in their national stadium. Just in case you're not a football historian and unaware of who won the Jules Rimet trophy in '66, I'll tell you the world champions that year were England, as this fact seems to have been brushed under the carpet and is very rarely mentioned in the media over the last five decades.

I'm not stating this tenuous link as a Sassenach having some kind of dig on our nation's only success in a book on Scottish football, because you'd be surprised to learn that as far as international football is concerned, Scotland was once my number one team.

I was 8 years old when I became football mad and my first World Cup was the 1974 tournament in West Germany.

The Scots were the only home nation that qualified and I keenly followed their progress along with marvelling the skills of Lorimer, Bremner, Dalglish and big Joe Jordan. The Scots were unbeaten in the group stage, including drawing with Brazil, but failed to progress because they basically could only score twice against a comical Zaire side, so went home on goal difference.

When the next tournament came around four years later in Argentina, yet again England declined to take part leaving the Tartan Army as the only British representatives in South America. I was more keen this time around, as I had a picture of Kenny Dalglish on my bedroom wall and I even bought that naff Rod Stewart World Cup record *Ole Ola,* so I was well up for it, especially after manager Ally McLeod declared that Scotland were going to win it. The tournament was a calamity both on and on the pitch, but at least there was the delight of Archie Gemmill's goal against Holland - the best goal I've ever seen.

The 1982 finals in Spain were great, not only did England finally get in on the act, but we had Northern Ireland to cheer on as well. Scotland of course kept up their fine record of qualifying, matched by their poor record of getting knocked out in the group phase. Nevertheless, I was so used to supporting that lot from 55 miles up the road that I bought a replica shirt to wear during the finals. I suppose I'm a bit old fashioned wanting the four nations and the Republic of Ireland to do well at tournaments, but my passport permits this right, it's just a shame that Scotland are now the ones that don't regularly participate every two summers.

Anyway, I digress, let's get back to 1966 and a wet Wednesday night on the 25th of May. The Scottish Junior

Cup final was an all eastern affair for the first time in 43 years as Bonnyrigg Rose playing out a 1-1 with Whitburn in front of a Hampden Park crowd of 19,450. After a tight encounter on the previous Saturday, the replay providing a record victory in the final - Bonnyrigg Rose 6 Whitburn Junior 1 - equalling the same score line set by Tranent when they gubbed Petershill in 1935.

Bonnyrigg Rose Athletic F.C. was founded in 1881 from Bonnyrigg Swifts who trace their origins back to 1874. The Rose have a long proud history of winning honours within the Junior ranks, with that '66 success followed by a second Junior Cup, when they defeated Stonehouse Violet 1-0 in 1978. In between those two victories they reached the final in 1972, after a 1-1 draw with Cambuslang Rangers they lost out to the best team of this era 3-2 in the replay.

The club won their first league title in the Edinburgh & District League in 1937–38, but it wasn't until 1963–64 that they repeated that achievement, before going onto win the East Region Division One in 1975–76, 1976–77 and again in 1984–85. They currently play in the SJFA East Region Super League and when I visited in May 2013 they were title holders, winning their second league championship following on for their initial success in 2008-09.

The Rose have also added a stack of cup honours, winning their first piece of silverware in the East of Scotland Junior Cup in 1898, which they've achieved a further six times, the last of which came a few weeks after my appearance at New Dundas Park. The club have also won the Brown Cup eight times and the East Junior League Cup on five occasions.

In September 2009, a new community club was formed - Bonnyrigg Rose Football (Sports) Club. The new club involves the amalgamation of Bonnyrigg Rose Boys Club, Bonnyrigg Rose 'A' U21s and Bonnyrigg Rose Athletic Junior Football Club. The boys club was formed in 1995 and since the merger has grown into one of the biggest clubs in the Midlothian area with teams of both sexes aged 8 - 16, with approximately 250 players registered.

For what was my one hundredth match of the 2012-13 season, again I met up with James for ... yes ... you guessed it ... my last day trip of the season. The fixtures for Saturday 18th May were released on the previous weekend, so after weighing up the options we decided to plump for Bonnyrigg Rose v Hill of Beath Hawthorn in the Fife and Lothians Cup, another pot the Rose have added to their honours list, winning the trophy in 1982, 2005 and 2007.

On arrival in Edinburgh it was absolutely lashing it down. The rain didn't ease up as I did my usual Edinburgh route before meeting James outside Waverley Station at 1245. When his car pulled up I was soaked to the skin and I was expecting to be greeted with news that our game was off, but to my surprise it was OK with apparently only one postponement in the area. It's common knowledge that as well as collecting football grounds I also like to bag Weatherspoon's pubs. I've logged them for several years now, making sure wherever I may wander there's a pre-match 'Spoons tour. On our way to the match we stopped off in Dalkeith to visit the only one in Midlothian - 'The Blacksmith's Forge' After the match we returned to Edinburgh via Musselburgh to tick off the impressive 'The David Macbeth Moir' - the only JDW in East Lothian.

Bonnyrigg is a town in Midlothian, found eight miles south-east of Edinburgh city centre. The town has been known as Bonnyrigg since the 1850s, but early maps show different spellings. In 1766 a village called "Bannockrigg" is shown in the locality, then the spelling changes to "Bannocrig" in 1815 which remained for almost 40 years, then for reasons unknown it changed again to the now familiar Bonnyrigg.

The town merged with the fellow burgh of Lasswade in 1929, becoming Bonnyrigg & Lasswade until the burgh was abolished in 1974. Bonnyrigg was a mining village until the 1920s, while its main industry was carpet making until the factory closed in 1978 after over 100 years in the business.

Bonnyrigg Rose had a world-famous star amongst their former players, a 6' 2" right winger who wore the red and white hooped shirt at the beginning of the 1950s. The former number 7 was apparently good enough to earn a trial with East Fife and knocked back an offer from Sir Matt Busby at Man United to concentrate on acting, so "who ish thish famoush shtar?" – his name is Connery, Sean Connery. The original and some still say the best actor to play the role of 007 James Bond on the big screen.

New Dundas Park was originally purchased by the Trustees of Bonnyrigg Rose Athletic F.C. from Sir Hendry Dundas and his mother Dame Jean Hood for £500 on the 10th June 1953. The main features are all found at the ground entrance side. The popular standing area has terrace steps fully covered running half pitch length, with a smaller open terrace in the centre facing the dugouts opposite. There are four cabins; a hospitality room, refreshment bar, referee's room/toilet block and a club shop. The far side has grass banking with three red crash barriers on the steeper side of the dugouts. The ground also has a distinct slope running across the pitch towards the dugout side, so overall a neat little ground which has greatly improved in recent years since the old pavilion burned down in September 2009.

As for the game, the home side dominated throughout, but as we reached the later stages of the game a penalty shoot-out looked on the cards as Rose continued to waste several gold glinted chances. The deadlock was finally broken in the 70th minute when Sean Grady headed home a lovely left wing cross from Gemmell, then a cracking chest and volley combo from Kris Renton on 82 minutes appeared to have booked a cup semi-final place. However, two minutes later the visitors replied, when sub Ross Allum latched onto a loose ball in the box to fire home and put Hawthorn back in the tie. This proved to be a temporary relapse as the impressive Renton added his second, firing a deflected assisted shot from the edge of the box in injury time. The victory was giving added gloss when a clumsy trip on Gemmell in the box saw Paul Currie convert from the penalty-spot, the fifth goal in a hectic last quarter of the match.

I left home that morning at 8 o'clock and got a thorough soaking in the torrential rain just walking to the bus stop. When I arrived in Edinburgh I couldn't believe that the downpour was just as heavy, so all day I looked like a drowned rat, finally feeling warm and dry on my return home twelve hours later. Although it was a rotten day weather wise I can't really complain, a new ground, two new Weatherspoon's pubs and some new additions to my vinyl vault.

From one Rose to another, and a trip to one of the most successful Junior clubs in the East Region of Scotland. Linlithgow Rose have won the prestigious cup on four occasions, the first of which came just before I was born in 1965, when goals from Oliphant, Grant, Cowie and Gardner saw The Gallant Rosey Posey stroll to a 4-1 win over Baillieston. They lost the final to Cambuslang Rangers in 1974, then had to wait until the new millennium before their next final appearance, making up for lost time as they reached the final five times in eleven years. In 2002 a goal by James Creaney was enough to overcome Auchinleck Talbot at Firhill Park, but they couldn't achieve the double as they lost out to Tayport the following year in extra time. The maroon ribbons adorned the old trophy again in 2007 in a closely fought contest with Kelty Hearts. The final took place at East End Park in Dunfermline, where a handsome crowd of 9,300 saw Brian Carrigan give the Rose the lead but a late leveller meant the game was decided in extra time, when a late header by substitute Mark Whyte clinched a 2-1 victory.

The 2010 final against Largs Thistle was settled by a 30-yard screamer by Kevin Donnelly to bring the cup back to Prestonfield for the fourth time, however they were denied a fifth success in 2013 when Auchinleck Talbot scored the only goal of the game to revenge that 2002 defeat.

The club formed back in 1889, originally playing home matches at Captains Park. They won their first trophy in the Forth League in 1902, followed by more honours in the County Cup and St Michaels Cup while playing at this ground. Just before the First World War they moved to Upper Mains Park, winning the Lumley Cup in 1914. The reformation of the Junior set up in 1924-25 placed Rose in the West Lothian Junior League and the club comfortably won the championship in their debut season.

Another move a few hundred yards down the road to Lower Main Park in 1930, coincided with the club's leanest spell with no honours won throughout that decade. After the Second World War the club looked for a new ground, eventually purchasing land adjacent to the Glue Works in 1947 which they named Preston Park. The ground was renamed Prestonfield two years later and it's been their home ever since with the ground's record attendance of 3,626, recorded for a game against Petershill in the late '60s.

Rose were Edinburgh League winners in four consecutive years from 1965 and were dominant in the East Region League, lifting their first of nine Division One championships in 1974-75. When I visited Linlithgow Rose in November 2013 they were the current East Super League champions (recurring theme happening here) winning the title for a third-time following success in 2004 and 2007. They are also the holders of the Fife & Lothians Cup which was won for the fifteenth time. Their excessive trophy haul also includes 14 East of Scotland Cup's, 10 East League Cup wins, a dozen successes in the St Michael's Cup and lifting the Brown Cup on eight occasions.

The Royal Burgh in West Lothian is famous for its loch and Linlithgow Palace, the home of the Stuart kings. After a disastrous fire in 1424 destroyed most of the town, the present palace was built by James I of Scotland and became the birthplace of James V and Mary Queen of Scots. In January 1746 troops of the duke of Cumberland's army marched out of the palace leaving fires burning which soon caught hold of the building and burnt it out, and ever since the palace has remained unroofed and uninhabited.

Another tourist attraction next to the Palace is St. Michael's Church, one of the largest burgh churches in Scotland the 15th century building is named after the town's patron saint; the Linlithgow motto is "St Michael is kind to strangers".

I arrived just before noon after catching the first available connection from Edinburgh. As I was still feeling slightly rough from being on the lash the previous night, I took a stroll down the High Street, along the loch and up to the palace. Once the cobwebs had blown off I still had enough time for a couple of pints before the 1.45pm kick off, calling at the GBG listed Platform 3 and The Four Marys.

I then took a walk up to the ground which at the time the best Scottish Junior ground I had visited. Prestonfield is dominated by the eye-catching Davy Roy Stand, which sits proudly on the halfway line. The stand has elevated seating under a cantilever roof, with standing room, dugouts, club offices and changing facilities underneath. The current maximum capacity of the ground is 3,500 with 301 maroon and white flip seats in the stand.

There are two turnstile entrances, one in the car park next to the Linlithgow Rose Social Club and the other at the top end of the ground. In between the two entrances are terracing with a covered centre paddock, with grass banking at the top goal which is a popular vantage point. The refreshment bar is at the back of the terrace and serves a great selection of savouries, including the delightful curry pie which was the 2013 winner of the 'Scabby-eye of the Year' award on my blog.

The 3rd round of the Scottish Junior Cup paired the Rosey Posey with the 2012 winners Shotts Bonn Accord. The hosts went into the game as favourites to progress but it was The Bonny who won for the first time at Prestonfield since 1962. There was a good crowd for the game including a decent away support and amongst the home fans was one man who must be the loudest bloke I've heard in my 40 years of attending football matches. This Rose supporter constantly shouted instructions throughout the game, every kick, every tackle, every decision, he made Neil Warnock sound like a shy little schoolboy. He even got a mentioned by one of the Rose players in the new club magazine 'The Gallant' and it comes as no surprise that he is nicknamed "Coach"

Shotts were the better side in a tight first half and should have took an early lead when a Chris Walker header struck the crossbar. However, they gained the advantage five minutes before half time, when McKenna robbed the defender and found Andy Cross who was left unmarked and finished well with just the goalkeeper to beat.

Rose worked hard to draw level but the Shotts defence held firm and added to their lead just minutes after a Smith effort hit the crossbar which denied Rose an equaliser. A long ball found McKenna who stayed onside, before finding McStay who played the ball out to Cross who fired in his second goal with a left foot shot. With time running out substitute Gordon Herd halved the deficit, firing home after a goalmouth scramble but the chance of a replay was never likely as Shotts seen out the final ten minutes and deservedly booked their place in the fourth round of the Junior Cup.

So, a good game and a thoroughly enjoyable afternoon. The match was a typical cup tie, the ground is a belter and the half time pie was top notch, so what's not to like? Hopefully more of the same coming up over the next year and a half on my trail of the Scottish Holy Grail. So far, I have been to five cup winners and for the record have also been to Newtongrange Star, Tranent Juniors, Dunbar United, the defunct Ballingry Rovers and Lewis United in the North Region. So, an overall total of only ten, however this tally is set to soar as my new obsession of completing another set gets underway in 2015.

Matchday Stats

Saturday 18th May 2013 (2pm ko)

Fife & Lothian Cup Quarter Final

Bonnyrigg Rose 4(Grady 70 Renton 82 90+1 Currie 90+3pen)

Hill of Beath Hawthorn 1(Allum 84)

Att.150.est   Ground no.351

Saturday 30th November 2013 (1.45pm ko)

Scottish Junior Cup 3rd Round

Linlithgow Rose 1(Herd 80)

Shotts Bonn Accord 2(Cross 39,65)

Att.600.est   Ground no.376

5 Let's Make Some Plans

(January 2015)

The new year is neither an end nor a beginning but merely a going on. Well it is when it comes to football. So as season 2014-15 kicks off for the second half, Newcastle United's season is already over, out of the FA Cup and still without a manager and Gateshead's chances of reaching the play-offs look more remote with every passing week. So, in these first few days of 2015 my mind is fully focused on future trips to Scotland and how many of the remaining 22 grounds I can tick off this season.

As I mentioned in the first chapter, I only have one work free Saturday per month plus a holiday entitlement of six weeks. Having already made plans for holidays and weekend breaks long before I came up with this concept, I'm only left with three blank Saturday's in January, February and May. I won't be happy going to just three grounds this season, I need to do at least double that amount, so it looks like I'll have to call in a few favours at work. On the subject of that four-letter word I better fill you in on my career. Since January 1988 I've worked for Royal Mail as a community communications officer, which sounds like a very important and interesting job. However, that's just my clever way of telling you that I'm a Postman, having delivered to nearly every home and business in Gateshead during my distinguished career. Nowadays you'll find me delivering inside the Metrocentre, having the honour of delivering the post in the biggest shopping precinct in Europe.

There's other viable options with midweek games at the end of the season and the Junior Cup semi-finals are sometimes played on a Sunday, so that means I could maybe get a least half a dozen clubs marked off before the SJFA season concludes in June.

Travelling to games shouldn't be too much of a problem as the Scottish Junior Cup has been dominated by the West Region over the last half a century, with 18 different winners in and around Glasgow in Renfrewshire, Lanarkshire with seven in Ayrshire, making it the most dominant county in Scotland. This means my most likely regular rail route is from Newcastle to Edinburgh on the East Coast line then across to Glasgow. or over to Carlisle, then onwards to Ayrshire or the west coast Euston to Glasgow Central service.

As far as the East Region is concerned there's been ten winners, and as I've already been to four of those this leaves just two in West Lothian, 3 in Fife and the furthest club north is Carnoustie Panmure in Angus. The cup hasn't been won by a North Region club since Bank 'O Dee triumphed in 1957, so on a personal level this has worked out great and made my task slightly easier, with the only awkward journeys being at Glenrothes, Tayport and the aforementioned Carnoustie.

At this point I must mention the Junior Cup winners who are unfortunately no longer with us. Baillieston FC beat Benburb in the 1980 final after a second replay. The club was formed in 1919 reaching their first final in 1924, losing to Parkhead and made a second unsuccessful appearance in 1965 against Linlithgow Rose. Their greatest era came in the early 80's when the club reached three Junior Cup finals in the space of five years, but one victory as they again lost out to Blantyre Victoria in 1982 and Bo'ness United in 1984. The club sold their Station Park ground to a developer in 2000 with the aim of moving to a purpose-built stadium in the Easterhouse area of Glasgow. After initially ground sharing and later playing all matches away, the proposed planned ground never materialised, so the club effectively dissolved in 2005, however the Baillieston Juniors name is kept alive by local youth sides.

As things stand I'm awaiting the fixtures for the 24th January which is an obstacle as the Junior fixtures are done in the making it up as you go along style, so mapping out fixtures well in advance is a nonstarter. The Junior Cup always takes priority with postponed matches and replays played the following Saturday, so with the 4th round taking place on the 17th I'm hoping to catch a replay or a rearranged game.

About making it up as you go along, this book is now up to date with the five grounds I've already visited covered over the previous three chapters, so at this point the future remains unwritten.

The working title is 'From the Toon to the Scottish Joons' which has a nice ring to it, but I'm still not too sure at this stage. As I live in Gateshead it should really be from the Heed to the Scottish Joons, but that obviously doesn't rhyme. I'll have to run the idea past a few of my Groundhopping pals in Scotland first, although after travelling to 22 grounds, I may accidently stumble upon a book title.

So as things stand at the beginning of the year when I hit the big five O, I'm looking to do six grounds in the second half of this season (before my birthday) and hopefully a dozen next season when I'll be fully focused on the task ahead. This will leave just four to do at the beginning of 2016-17 season, although there could be a couple of more grounds if the 2015 and 2016 winners are clubs which haven't previously lifted the trophy during my lifetime. My overall aim is to finish this latest list and this book by Christmas 2016, so here we go ... 22 grounds in 22 months.

6. Steeltown

Kilbirnie Ladeside - Valefield Park (January 2015)

Last Saturday was the Scottish Junior Cup 4th Round, 16 ties were scheduled to take place but due to the invasion of the familiar white cold stuff there wasn't a ball kicked in anger. This was of course good news on my part, as it was looking good to catch a preferred big cup tie to get things rocking and rolling.

After surveying the fixtures, I decided on the tie between Arthurlie and Kirkintilloch Rob Roy as the destination of choice to get this show on the road. I prepared as I always do by researching the place and history of the club for my blog, but my plans begun to look a bit iffy after another midweek snowfall, however I remained optimistic as the weather forecast was very good with exotic temperatures of 6 Celsius for the weekend.

On the Wednesday night, I booked trains from Carlisle to Glasgow, but my plans were again buggered as engineering works on the Newcastle to Carlisle route, meant a replacement bus service from Hexham, which added an extra 40 minutes onto the journey. I decided that it was more easier and much quicker to drive along to Carlisle myself and jump the train to Glasgow from there, which unfortunately would restrict my intake of alcohol.

On Friday night, I sent a tweet to Arthurlie inquiring about the pitch and the chances of the game going ahead, which they replied to straight away saying the chances were 50-

50 but they remained hopeful. As a precaution, I had another look at the fixtures and worked out which grounds were possible within the timescale of getting to and from Glasgow Central between noon and 4.30. I jumped into the car on Saturday morning to head west to Cumbria, not knowing where my destination would be, just a list of travel details for seven possibilities which all added to the excitement.

I parked up in Carlisle at 1025 and immediately checked my phone for messages to find out what was on and off. I received a tweet from Brian, a Kirkintilloch Rob Roy fan who informed me that the Arthurlie match was postponed. Paisley based Chris Sanderson kept me well informed throughout the morning, confirming that a few of my options and my main back up plan of Kilbirnie Ladeside v Kilsyth Rangers was on.

Typically, the national train provider on the west side of the country yet again let me down, giving me another kick in the jewels with the 1047 running 35 minutes late. I don't know if it's just me being unlucky or if they're frequently so incompetent. For legal reasons, I won't mention the name of the company, I'll just give you a clue that it shares its name with the Madonna hit from 1985, you know the one I mean, the song when she felt like she'd been touched for the very first time.

Thankfully there was a regular service for my onward journey to Glengarnock, the nearest rail station to the ground so after checking my notes I knew I had just enough time to buy my tickets and catch the 1248 which took around 25 minutes, so nicely timed to arrive in time for the 1.45 kick off.

After arriving at Glengarnock it was just a 10-minute stroll up to Kilbirnie, which is a wee town situated in the Garnock Valley area of North Ayrshire, around 20 miles south-west of Glasgow and approximately 10 miles from Paisley. The town was historically built up around the flax and weaving industries before the Glengarnock Steel Works opened its blast furnaces around 1841. The works closed in 1985, and nowadays the area has very few local employers, making it more of a commuter town to the nearby bigger towns and cities.

Kilbirnie Ladeside formed in 1901 and are nicknamed The Blasties, which derives not just from the steel works but from a Robert Burns poem, The Inventory, written in 1786. The poem refers to the local Saint Brennan's Day Fair, the largest horse market in the west of Scotland and his purchase of a plough horse; My furr-ahin 's a wordy beast, As e'er in tug or tow was traced. The fourth's a Highland Donald hastle, A damn'd red-wud Kilburnie blastie!

The club won the Junior Cup twice, in 1952 with a 1-0 win over Camelon, before having to wait a quarter of a century when featuring in the very first Scottish Junior Cup Final on TV (STV) when they beat Kirkintilloch Rob Roy 3-1 at Hampden Park in front of a crowd of 11,476. This was also the year of the Queen's Silver Jubilee, when we each received a commemorative silver coin from school and in '77 I got my first spiky haircut, modelled in the style of Bruce Foxton from The Jam, which is a hairstyle which has basically stuck with me for much of the last 40 years. Kilbirnie also reached the final in 1987 but were denied the Junior Cup hat-trick after drawing 1-1 with Auchinleck Talbot they narrowly lost the replay 1-0.

I arrive at the ground at 1.30 and was quite impressed with Valefield Park. There are two enclosures at the Kirkland Road side of the ground, both identical with one of the stands having a small section of wooden seat benches and some impressive terracing behind the goals.

This tie was one of only five cup games to beat the weather with the Vale pitch looking in great nick, considering it was still under a blanket of snow in the middle of the week. The Blasties faced First Division side Kilsyth Rangers in a match which turned out to be a closely fought contest, although the score line would suggest otherwise.

Kilbirnie took the lead after just nine minutes when Richie Barr raced onto a through ball and calmly slotted home, but the Wee Gers were level on 24 minutes when Joe Barclay received the ball on the right flank before cutting inside and firing in from a tight angle.

The match was nicely poised at this stage but two goals before half time booked Ladeside's passage into round five. Just after the half hour mark a Wilson free kick from the right was nodded past his own 'keeper by David Water, the goal was quite bizarre as it looked as if he had forgotten he was defending and headed home like a top striker into the far corner, giving the 'keeper no chance.

Chris Sanderson had also sent me a twitter message advising me to watch the match in the shed with Kilbirnie nutcases who make a lot of noise and get right behind their team. The nutcases (his words not mine) gave the own goal victim plenty of abusive stick and his response to the crowd was to give them the international signage of "f**k off you wankers" by doing the knuckle shuffle gesture through a grimaced face.

Just before the break a long through ball found both Ryan Borris and Christopher Craig in acres of space. The linesman flagged for offside but the referee waved play on before Borris teed up his teammate up for a simple finish.

At the interval, I devoured a mince pie and a coffee and made my way to the stands to watch the second half next to...but not amongst... the club's noisiest supporters, realising at this point that I was the only spectator in the vicinity without a can of lager in my hand.

The visitors made an encouraging start to the second half and if they'd a been a bit more clinical in front of goal they could have easily drawn level. They were made to pay for those missed chances as the hosts sealed the win when a quick break from midfield was finished off by Ryan Borris, before a late consolation from Barclay made the score line look a bit more respectable in a typical end-to-end cup tie.

After the game, I ran down to the station to catch the connection back to Glasgow. The earlier train delay was the only downer on a cracking day, which meant I didn't have much leisure time in Glasgow, although I did have a 20-minute window on the way home to pop into Frop on Union Street to bag a copy of the new Belle & Sebastian LP. I shouldn't be too disappointed as there'll be plenty of other opportunities to have time for a bevvy in Glasgow as my latest groundhopping pursuit will see becoming a regular visitor to the west of Scotland, as it's the most successful region for Junior Cup winners, and Kilbirnie is just the first of many cracking grounds to come.

Matchday Stats

<u>Saturday 24th January 2015 (1.45pm ko)</u>

Scottish Junior Cup 4th Round

Kilbirnie Ladeside 4(Barr 9 Waters 32OG Craig 44 Borris 75)

Kilsyth Rangers 2(Barclay 24,89)

Att.300est

Ground no.433

7. A Heady Tale

Shotts Bon Accord - Hannah Park (February 2015)

Prior to visiting a new football ground I always research the town and the club in question, as a prologue to my matchday reports on my blog. So, during my years of groundhopping my geography knowledge and the history of the backwaters of the UK is now up to A Level standard.

I do like a good historic fact and an informative piece of local folklore, a superb example being a tale from the 15th century about the legendary giant Bertram de Shotts. Bertram was a big bloke, somewhere in between seven to eight feet tall, which is huge when you compare it to the average height of a man around this period, which would have been a wee bit short of five and a half feet. Shotts roamed the moorland where he was notorious for mugging pack men and peddlers as they carried their goods back and forwards along the Great Road of the Shire. His ferocious actions came to the attention of King James IV of Scotland, who became so peeved off with the big fella's antics that he offered a large reward for his death.

Bertram's life came to a barbaric ending in a gripping tale told by Willielmo, the 1st Laird of Muirhead who slayed the giant, ambushing and paralyzed him by slicing both his hamstrings as he lay down to drink at Kate's Well in Sallysburgh (which is now Salsburgh, 3 miles from Shotts) He was then savagely decapitated with De Muirhead proudly carrying the bloodied head to the King, claiming his reward of a 'Hawk's Flight' of land, which subsequently became the Muirhead's Lauchope estate.

Bertram de Shotts lived roughly between 1467 to 1505 and the village of Shotts is believed to be named after the renowned giant. However boring Toponymies maintain that the name derives from the Anglo-Saxon word - 'sceots' (steep slopes) as the real origin of the name, but the legend of Bertram de Shotts is a much better source and a splendid tale in the history of this part of Lanarkshire.

The area originally consisted of five villages - Dykehead, Calderside, Springhill, Torbothie and Stane with the focus being the works area of Calderside. The villages of Allanton, Hartwood and Eastfield are now deemed as being Shotts, so nowadays the population is just over 8,000. The small rural town was renowned for its mining and ironworks, having 22 coal mines dotted around the area prior to the Second World War, with Northfield Colliery being the last to close in the 1960s.

My two recent trips to Scotland have seen me end up at a different match to the one initial intended. I fully expected my planned trip this week to Shotts Bon Accord to again fall foul to the weather, so I was well prepared with a list of potential backups. Last week my new year plan to tick off at least half a dozen this season took a setback, as my trip to Hill of Beath Hawthorn was postponed due to frost. After checking the remaining fixtures the clubs on my list were either playing away or it was logistically impossible to get across to the West Region in time for kick off. I still managed to get to a game and a new ground though, ringing my Edinburgh pal Jamie McQueen who issues the matchday programme and is also a committee member at

Whitehill Welfare. So instead of a Junior tick it was Lowlands League action, with Jamie giving me a lift down to the village of Rosewell in Midlothian, where I saw the Welfare put up a disappointing display to lose 2-1 to Stirling University.

One of my greatest traits is the ability to remember dates, I never forget birthdays or anniversaries and a particular date sticks in my mind as a reference to an attended match. Take for example the date of this game - the 28th February which I automatically connected with my first ever away match and a first visit to the Wembley Empire Stadium. The occasion was the 1976 League Cup Final - Manchester City v Newcastle United, a memorable day travelling down the A1 with my Dad in his Austin 1100. The match was a classic northern encounter, but the result was disappointing as United lost 2-1, but put up a fine performance in comparison to their previous visit to Wembley two years earlier. I saw Newcastle United play a total of five times at the old Wembley, with my matchday statistics being ... Won 0 Drew 0 Lost 5 Goals for 2 Goals against 12, so as you can imagine the Toon Army weren't too bothered when they pulled the bugger down!

And so, to my latest matchday on the last non-leap year day of February. Shotts is located almost halfway between Glasgow and Edinburgh. It would have been easier to travel to the town from the capital, but as today's fixtures were just published last week, I had already trousered advanced train tickets to Glasgow.

I arriving mid-morning, which allowing plenty of time to visit my favourite shopping outlets and of course have a few bevvies. Breakfast was partaking in the Camperdown Place Weatherspoon's, which still has black pudding on the breakfast menu, but my delight was dampened by the fact they don't serve alcohol until 11am.

One of my favourite shops in Glasgow is 'Missing' which is an Aladdin's Cave for collectors like myself, having a huge range of CD's, DVD's, vinyl, football programmes and magazines, autographs, basically a shitload of great stuff! I picked up a couple of CD's for only two quid a piece (old albums by Stephen Malkmus and Flaming Lips) and headed off for a few pints.

After a swift pint in The Crystal Palace, where I rang the club secretary just to confirm the match was on, I surveyed a couple of boozers for future visits to Glasgow, calling into The Horse Shoe bar, which is a cracking boozer and the Drum & Monkey, before catching the 1 o' clock train.

The train journey was nicely timed so I arrived at Hannah Park ten minutes before kick-off. The ground appears as a huge venue, having one the largest playing surfaces at this level surrounded by an oval track. There is a central standing enclosure on one side, with eight steps of terracing which snakes around the other three sides of the ground. The brick wall around the perimeter of the terraces forms the dugouts at the far side.

The 4,000-capacity ground was built by the workforce of local volunteers and is named in honour of James Hannah, who died of thrombosis contracted during the efforts to finish the ground. As well as being a football stadium, it's also been used as the venue of the annual Shotts Highland Games.

Shotts Bon Accord FC were formed and began playing in the Lanarkshire League in 1950. The club were one of the most successful in the competition, winning the title for the first time in 1957-58, in the same season they won their first Scottish Junior Cup, by beating Pumpherston 2-0 in front of a 33,000 crowd at Hampden Park. Six further league titles followed during the 1960s, and they also lifted the League Cup on seven occasions, until the flagging league saw the remnant clubs move into the Central League from the 1968-69 season.

During their time in the Central League, The Bonny played within its three divisions, most which in its Premier Division, until the club fell out with the game's governing body and were suspended in 1995. The club returned to the league the following year and placed in its third tier. Under the helm of new manager Rab Sneddon they won a hat-trick of championships in all three divisions, crowned Premier Division winners in 1998-99.

The amalgamation of the Ayrshire League and the Central League at the end of the 2001/02 season, saw Shotts enter the Superleague First Division for the following campaign. In 2004-05 they won promotion to the top division after finished runners-up to Kilsyth Rangers.

The long awaited second success in the Junior Cup finally came in 2012, beating warm favourites Auchinleck Talbot at Almondvale Stadium, with goals from McCluskey and Boyack securing a 2-1 win. I must also add that this fine club has got nowt to do with the Bon Accord that lost 36-0 to Arbroath in 1885, that club were from Aberdeen not North Lanarkshire.

On arrival I was greeted by Alec Hendry who apologised for not asking who I was when I rang him earlier, and he invited me upstairs in the clubhouse for a cup of tea and a chat at half time. Everyone was very hospitable and recognized my presence, even when I bought a pie and a pin badge at the Bonny Bisto I was kindly giving me a couple of old programmes, which included both Shotts recent Junior Cup semi-finals.

Prior to this game, I fully expected Shotts in their traditional all maroon kit to comfortably book their place in the next round of the West of Scotland Cup, however Vale of Clyde can count themselves unlucky not to have at least taking the tie to penalties. They took the lead in the 27th minute when a cross from the right dropped onto the left foot of Higgins who hit a half volley out of the reach of Whyte, but unfortunately the visitors couldn't keep hold of their slim advantage and ten minutes later the Bonny equalised with a quite bizarre goal. The ball found the back of the net at the third attempt, after the initial shot from Marriott hit the underside of the crossbar and bounced in front of Allan McCrum, his point-blank effort well saved, but Jordan White was on hand to fire home the rebound.

At the beginning of the second half the visitors made a substitution. I won't embarrass the player in question by naming him, but as I'm a betting man I would confidently wager that this bloke has never been out of Scotland in his life. Honestly, he was the whitest man I've ever seen, with a pair of legs resembling two bottles of puro sterilised milk! This distraction didn't draw my attention away from a finely poised tie, with the best chance of the second half saw a header from Chris Walker kicked off the line on 70 minutes which could have settled it. But just as it was looking like Vale had won a ticket for the spot kick lottery, a right-wing corner in the final minute saw Jack Marriott fire in through a crowded penalty area to book their place in round three.

After the game, I thanked Alec for a great afternoon and headed next door to the Shotts Bon Accord Social Club. Just as was leaving I was approached by a member of the football club hierarchy who apologised for not getting the chance to speak to me earlier, wishing me well and I promised to send him a copy of my book ... if it gets published.

The heavy rain which was forecast thankfully held off until the final whistle, so I got soaked running back down to the train station, but this didn't but the dampeners on what was an ace day. Shotts are a smashing club and even though the ground is notoriously known for its freezing cold conditions this didn't bother a proper Geordie like myself, but any southern shandy drinkers who may want to take a shot at visiting Shotts I would maybe best leave it until late May or early June.

Matchday Stats

Saturday 28th February 2015 (2pm ko)

New Coin Holdings Cup Round 2

Shotts Bon Accord 2(White 38 Marriott 89)

Vale of Clyde 1(Higgins 27)

Att. 90apx

Ground no.436

8. Blue Soap

Cambuslang Rangers - Somervell Park (March 2015)

The March football schedule is always a hectic part of the season. Over the last few weeks I've travelled down to Yorkshire a couple of times, been over to Belfast and last Saturday I made a 720-mile round trip to Dover. It was there in northern France that I witnessed the worst game I've seen this season, with the only decent effort on goal all afternoon finding the back of the Gateshead net.

Today was my third trip north of the border in the space of seven days, attending the Sunday leg of the Lowlands League Hop with two matches in Dumfries & Galloway. This was followed by the Scotland v Northern Ireland international friendly at Hampden on Wednesday night, in the company of Tony Carter and Simon Lowery, who are the two most devoted Heed Army foot soldiers in the whole world!

For my latest trip to Glasgow I wasn't a "William no mates" as my pal from work "Honest Paul" came along for the ride. I've known Paul since he started at Royal Mail in 2001 and we became good mates after it came to our attention we are both Morrissey fans. Our common fondness of quality music, plus a good day out on the lash, has meant we've been to a few gigs together over the years he's usually the first name on the list when I organise an all-day beano for the lads.

Football allegiances is also crucial when it comes to friendship, so thankfully he supports Newcastle and watches Gateshead occasionally. As for his musical taste, he's a huge Bowie fan, having seen "The Thin White Duke" on numerous occasions dating back to the 1970's. He also has a fondness for Roxy Music and as far as Scottish bands go, he adores The Associates, with the late Billy Mackenzie being one of his big musical heroes. If Paul accompanies me to more games you'll learn more about him as this book progresses, but here's a few snippets to be going on with; One of his best pals is former Middlesbrough and Liverpool striker David Hodgson. Their friendship goes way back to their schooldays and they still kept in touch when Hodgie became a big soccer star. Another good celebrity related fact is he kopped off with one of the lasses from 80's synth sensations The Human League. Not the blonde one (who was working as a waitress in a cocktail bar) but the dark haired one...no! not Phil Oakley, but the other backing singer, with the side parting and the massive beauty spot on her cheek. He gets the name "Honest Paul" because he was a bookie, not a proper Turf Accountant but someone you could lay a bet with at work. Nowadays with the convenience of mobile betting, chucking on a late wager is a simple task so Paul's services aren't required as much, compared to over a decade ago when not many people knew his real name, just simply known as "Ladbrokes".

We left Newcastle on the 7.43 to Edinburgh, then following a quick train swap we arrived in Glasgow at 10.25. The journey between Edinburgh and Glasgow was pretty stressful, as my Scottish Joons twitter feed list saw the fixtures in the West Region dropping like flies after a night of heavy rain. I was expecting to yet again look for an alternative match, but as I was enjoying my first drink of the day in the Camperdown Place the news came from the Wishaw Juniors feed that the match was on.

Cambuslang is just an eight-minute train journey from Glasgow Central, so we enjoyed a few pints before heading to the game, calling into the Counting House, The Society Rooms and the Crystal Palace before catching the 1250 service. As well as bagging football grounds and accumulating vinyl, another thing I collect is JD Weatherspoon's pubs, so on arrival we headed straight to the impressive new 'spoons in the town; The John Fairweather on Main Street which was a picture house in its previous life was my 231st pub in my never-ending Weatherspoon's UK tour.

Cambuslang is a suburban town located just south of the River Clyde, known as "the largest village in Scotland" with a population of around 24,500 and historical links to coal mining, iron and steelmaking.

Cambuslang is an ancient part of South Lanarkshire where Iron Age remains loom over modern day housing estates. Due to its location, the town has been very prosperous over time, due to its agricultural land and mineral resources underfoot, such as limestone, iron and coal. This wealth was guarded by the medieval Church, and later by the local upper classes, particularly the Duke of Hamilton. These riches made the town intimately concerned in the politics of the country and over the centuries the Church has made Cambuslang a major focal point.

The manufacturing industries attracted workers from the rest of Scotland, Ireland and other European countries. This diverse population increase posed problems in housing, employment and education, although

Cambuslang has always benefited from its closeness to the thriving city of Glasgow. The two brought closer in the 18th century by a turnpike road then of course the railway and nowadays wider communication networks, particularly the M74 motorway.

The town was represented at the start of the Scottish Football League in 1890-91. Cambuslang FC were founder members but folded after just two seasons in the new league, their most notable achievement being runners-up in the Scottish Cup in 1888.

Cambuslang Rangers were originally known as Leeside and joined the Junior ranks in 1892, changing their name to Clyde Rovers. They changed to their present handle in 1899 and changing their kit from red and white to Royal Blue to become "The Wee Gers".

They joined the Glasgow and District Junior League in 1900-01, winning their first trophy as champions in 1901-02 before repeating the feat the following year. The club switched to the Glasgow League in 1904, winning the title in 1911, 1912 and 1916 and finished that decade by reaching their first Junior Cup final in 1920, losing to Parkhead 2-0.

In 1927 they again lost out in the Junior Cup final to Glencair, but made it third time lucky in 1938 defeating Benburb 3-2 at Celtic Park. When football resumed after the Second World War they got to another final, but were defeated 3-1 by Burnbank Athletic. During the 1950s and 60s the club few minor cup honours and lost two more Junior finals against Dunbar United in 1961 and Johnstone Burgh in '64

After a thirty year wait the Scottish Junior Cup was finally brought back to Somervell Park, when they defeated

Kirkintilloch Rob Roy 1-0 in the 1969 final at Hampden Park. This was a significant year in my own life as it holds my first childhood memory. On a wet Wednesday afternoon on the 11th of September my sister was born. Just like my own birthday four years earlier my mother chose to have a home birth, so I was sent around to my Nanna's for a few hours and returned home to discover a baby sister, who I named Gillian. As much as I love my only sibling, when the year 1969 is ever mentioned I don't think of my brains oldest recollection, my mind automatically thinks this was the year when Newcastle United last lifted a trophy. After overcoming some of the top clubs in Europe, United lifted the Inter-Cities Fairs Cup after a 6-3 aggregate win over Hungarian giants Ujpest Dozsa. If you have bought this book for a couple of bob in a charity shop many years after it was published, then it's more than likely that this unwanted fact is still relevant today.

Winning the Junior Cup again heralded a golden era for The Wee Gers, as they went on to beat Newtongrange Star 2-1 in the 1971 final and retained the trophy with a 3-2 win over Bonnyrigg Rose after a replay. This was the first time a club had back-to-back wins in this century and they almost made it a hat-trick, but were thwarted by Irvine Meadow, losing 1-0 in the second replay.

Cambuslang earned the title of "Junior Side of the Century" by the Scottish Newspapers, as during this era they were also winning an array of league titles and cup honours. The Lang added the top prize yet again to regain the Scottish Junior Cup with a 3-1 win over Linlithgow Rose in 1974. Since that golden era silverware has been hard to come by, although they did win the 2nd Division of the Central League in 1989-90 and the Division One title the following season. At the time of my visit they were playing in the Central District Second Division.

Somervell Park is just across the road from the rail station although after a few pints I somehow forgot this fact and continued walking further away from the ground until realising my mistake and retraced my steps. We entered the turnstiles just as the referee was getting the match underway. The club have played at the ground since 1904, where there's a standing enclosure about two-thirds pitch length with eight large steps of terracing which runs around the other three sides. The dugouts are opposite built into the perimeter wall. The changing rooms and food hut are at the corner entrance next to Sweepers Lounge Bar and the open elements give panoramic views of Glasgow.

Cambuslang were up against Wishaw in the 2nd round of the Central League Cup. The match came to a grinding half with just a few minutes gone, when Wishaw's Gerry Ward went down injured after an early corner kick. There was a long delay before the player was finally removed from the pitch and rushed to hospital with a suspected broken ankle. Thankfully the injury wasn't as serious as first thought, it was just severely bruised, with the Wishaw Twitter page warning Gerry that there was to be no dancing on Saturday night. When the game finally got into its stride it was the visitors who were the better side throughout the first half, after going behind to an early strike from Grant Howarth, who cheekily lobbed the 'keeper from the edge of the box with just ten minutes gone. The match was a proper cup tie with plenty of take no prisoners challenges flying in, which Paul commented on saying "They narf get stuck in up here" After missing several good chances Wishaw finally levelled just before half time, when Chalmers received a left-wing cross to place his shot out of the goalkeepers reach from the edge of the box.

At half time, we went into Sweepers for a drink, which Paul described as looking like a nightclub. Although I failed to see the comparison I must say the toilets were quite flash, so I was expecting a big hefty black guy in there with a selection of after shaves and wet wipes, with me trying not to make eye contact in case he made the offer of. "would you like a freshening up sir?" Then reluctantly having to give him a pound coin for the privilege.

The second half was an even affair but Wishaw finished the game on top but were unable to grab the vital winner. The whistle blew with the teams still level, which meant no messing about with a replay or extra time, just straight onto the penalty kicks. The Wishaw players looked confident and on the match overall, they deserved their victory, with Sandy Thomson saving twice to win the penalty shootout by 3 strikes to 2.

The penalty shootout meant we missed the four o'clock train, but another soon arrived so we had a few more pub hours in Glasgow. One the city's bars which has become a favourite of mine is The Horseshoe Bar on Drury Street, which has a nice friendly atmosphere, serves a delicious pint of Harviestoun Bitter & Twisted and has free Wi-Fi - so what's not to like! Another pub we visited was the Pot Still, just around the corner on Hope Street. This cosy bar boasts a selection of over 600 whiskies, so after Paul got the round of beers in we looked around at this small cramped pub and noticed we were the only ones without a wee dram. In a moment of guilt and not wanting to be the odd couple, Paul asked if I wanted a whisky chaser, but I politely declined.

To allow ourselves more time in Glasgow we travelled back home via Carlisle, to catch the 2124 back to the Toon. We went on a crawl of the pubs closest to Carlisle station and enjoyed a hilarious and action packed ninety minutes. Although Paul is now in his mid-fifties he's a bit of a F-magnet with the women and if I wasn't already a happily married man I'm confident we could have easily pulled, as some of the flirty women we encountered seemed to have seen more sex than a coppers torch!

So overall a cracking day out which managed to tick all the right boxes which was topped off by our host club for the day - Cambuslang Rangers. While I was at the game I went to the food hut for a pie and a Bovril and asked the bloke who served me if they had any pin-badges. There were also two young lasses standing at the hut and one of them was sent away to find her Dad to see if he had any. A few minutes later the wee girl appeared with two different pin-badges, when I asked how much she said they were free. After I wrote my blog report, I learned that the gentleman who sent me the badges was Jim the club photographer. He thanked me for a cracking article but apologised for not making us more welcome, because if he had known how far we had travelled he would have offered us hospitality and introduced us to the club committee. This nice gesture means from now on I'll have to alert the clubs of my pending visit, not for the free cup of tea and custard creams, but to meet the people behind the scenes of these fabulous clubs.

Matchday Stats

<u>Saturday 28th March 2015 (2pm kick off)</u>

Euroscot Eng. Central League Cup Round 2

Cambuslang Rangers 1 (Howarth 8)

Wishaw Juniors 1(Charmers 45)

(Wishaw win 3-2 on penalties)

Att.160hc

Ground no.444

9. Top of the Pops

Auchinleck Talbot - Beechwood Park (April 2015)

If there was ever one precise example why I've fallen head over heels for the Junior game and made this the subject of my fitba book, then it's an occasion such as this. A fabulous ground within a scenic setting, with a big Junior Cup semi-final, embroidered in passion, commitment and drama, as Auchinleck Talbot the competition's most successful club faced the current cup holders Hurlford United.

I travelled via the Carlisle train route to the village situated at the heart of the ancient Kyle district of Ayrshire. The journey was a straightforward one, boarding the 0924 from Newcastle to Carlisle, then the slow train to Glasgow Central at 11.15, which takes the scenic route towards Gretna Green and Dumfries, then onwards through Ayrshire. I had half an hour spare in between trains but managed to resist a quick bevvy in Wetherspoon, to grab a bite to eat instead, plus I was still feeling a bit rough from the Newcastle Beer Festival the night before.

I arrived in Auchinleck at 1240. The town's name derives from Scottish Gaelic - achadh ('field') and leac ('slab') meaning a 'field of flat stones'. There are records of a community existing from the early 13th century, however the village came to prominence with arrival of the Boswell family in 1504. The marriage of a daughter of Sir John Auchinleck to Thomas Boswell, saw the estate and the title of laird granted to Boswell by King James IV. The family's diligence of their large estate saw the growth of a practical village community emerge from the surrounding barren moorland.

As you step off the train you're greeted by the sight of the Barony A frame tower. The village benefited from mining and quarrying in the area, which saw the population rise fourfold in fifty years to almost 7,000 by 1881. The Nationalisation of coal industry in 1947 brought investment, along with the building of the Barony Power Station in 1957. However, the village went into industrial decline after the demise of deep pit mining and the closure of the power station in 1989, and the tower remains as a monument to its proud heritage.

Surrounding the village is Auchinleck House, which is an 18th-century Category A listed mansion. The estate has the remains of Auchinleck Castle and Auchinleck Old House and it was the former home of the lawyer, diarist and biographer James Boswell, 9th Laird of Auchinleck. His biography of Dr. Samuel Johnson is regarded as an important stage in the development of the modern genre, claimed at the time as the greatest biography written in English. (until obviously, this book was published...Ed)

As there was a big crowd expected I headed straight to the ground as I wanted to take some photographs of a naked Beechwood Park for the blog. On my arrival, there were quite a few club staff already at the ground and I was made welcome and allowed a leisurely lap of snaps. Beechwood Park is dominated by the impressive main stand, which was opened in 2005 and sits half way with a mixture of 500 different coloured seats. There is terracing on all sides with a covered enclosure at the far side beyond the dugouts. The ground has some nice touches, painted in the black and gold club colours with the club crest embossed on the walls.

Auchinleck Talbot formed in 1909 and are named in honour of Lord Talbot de Maldahide, the man who gifted the club their Beechwood Park home. Due to financial problems Talbot folded in 1916 but returned four years later, winning the Ayrshire Cup with a 3-0 victory over Irvine Meadow. In 1920 they set a club goal scoring record in the Scottish Junior Cup, defeating Craigbank 11–0 at home, a score line they surpassed when hammering Nairn St. Ninian 13–1 in 2008.

Talbot are the most successful club in the history of the Scottish Junior Cup, lifting the trophy on ten occasions, stretching back to a 3-2 victory over Petershill in 1949. Their fantastic record in the competition is shown on the club crest, which (currently) has ten stars arched around a shield in the club colours of gold and black. They became the first club to lift the trophy in three consecutive years with a 3-2 win over Pollock in 1986, followed by single goal victories over Kilbirnie Ladeside and Petershill. At the turn of the 1990's they beat Newtongrange Star and Glenafton, with their next success coming 14 years later against Bathgate Thistle in the 2006 final. In recent years, they have been the team you must beat in the cup, with Talbot triumphant over Clydebank in 2009, Musselburgh Athletic in 2011 and Linlithgow Rose in 2013. The chance of another three in a row was denied after losing the 2012 final to Shotts Bon Accord.

It's not just the Junior Cup where honours have been won, there's also eleven Ayrshire League titles, three West of Scotland Super League Premier Division and they won the West of Scotland Cup nine seasons out of ten between 1979 and 1989, plus there's also an array of regional cup competitions to add to the trophy cabinet.

There was still plenty of spare time before the 2.30 kick off, so I called into the Boswell Arms at the end of the road for a pre-match pint. The bar was quite packed with a mix of both sets of supporters, with the away fans donning the red and white stripes of Hurlford United, not looking confident of retaining their crown against the kings of the Junior Cup. I then returned for a drink in the Supporters Social Club, ordering another pint of McEwans Export which has the famous laughing cavalier emblem, which I wanted to get tattooed on my arm but was severely warned against doing so by my adoring breadknife. I noticed that the locals call Mac Export "light" which is anything but in both appearance and taste. In the club, I met up with Donald McCrorie from the 100FgC Facebook group for a quick chat before the game. Donald lives in nearby Ochiltree and reports on the local Junior matches for Dirtytackle.net and the Ayrshire Post. He was telling me that there were quite a few fans from the other Ayrshire Junior clubs coming to lend their support to the Bot as they didn't want upstarts Hurlford United winning the cup.

The Bot went into the second leg with a handsome 3-1 lead from the first leg last Saturday and it seemed just a case of finishing off the job to reach their 13th Junior Cup final. As you can imagine there was a big crowd for the occasion and as I walked through the hefty throng I noticed quite a few heavily pregnant women. I wondered how there could be so many expectant mothers at the same time, before it suddenly dawned on me that if you count back 8 months it was the 2014 World Cup in Brazil, so the conception must have taken place whilst England were playing one of their three group matches.

Talbot had the best of the first half, applying pressure with a few decent headed efforts on goal but nothing clear cut in a disjointed opening period. The match sprang into life just two minutes after the restart in a crazy 10-minute spell as I was queuing up at the snack bar for a pie.

Talbot goalkeeper Andy Leishman brought down Ross Robertson in the box with the referee having no hesitation in awarding the penalty, followed by a straight red card. Without a substitute 'keeper it was left to Davy Gormley to don the goalie's gloves, and he miraculously pulled off a fabulous save to deny Stewart Kean from 12 yards. The save lead to a mad scramble in the six-yard box with the ball eventually put out for a corner and two players booked for playing a major part in the fracas.

From the resulting corner kick the ball was met at the far post by Robertson who headed home to put the Ford back in the tie. It was now game on with the visitors having the extra man advantage and facing an untried 'keeper between the sticks. That numerical edge didn't last much longer as two minutes later an ugly tackle from Kean meant a second yellow card, so we were back to level sides with still half an hour left to play.

This seemed to give the home side a major boost and they went onto win the tie with two individual pieces of brilliance. Just before the hour mark a Bryan Young in swinging corner swerved over the defence and directly into the far corner of the net to put his side level and restore the two-goal aggregate advantage.

Hurlford failed to test the stand in 'keeper and their grip on the trophy slipped away with an ambitious effort from Keir Milliken, striking his shot wide on the left and a few yards over the halfway line, sailed high, handsome and over the 'keeper and into the net. A truly wonderful strike and a fitting goal to book a place in another cup final, as The Bot look to extend their position as the top club in the number one position of most Junior Cup triumphs.

After the match, I walked alongside the jubilant supporters towards The Railway Inn which is the name suggests, is the closest pub to the station. The journey home was straight forward as well, due back in Newcastle nice and early at 2018. So, as I stood on the platform waiting for the 1708 and reflecting on a terrific afternoon's entertainment, it's at this point in the proceedings that this pleasant spring day in glorious warm Ayrshire sunshine went fat bottom over large bosom!

Auchinleck station is as remote and as basic as it gets, without any staff, electrical signage or tannoy announcer, just a board with a timetable on both platforms. Half an hour quickly passed without the murmur of a distant train, so one of my fellow patient passengers rang the control centre to find out what was happening. He was told there was a staff shortage so the train was cancelled, however they didn't seem too bothered to pass on this valuable piece of information on to the half a dozen commuters waiting patiently on platform 2. The next train wasn't due until twenty to seven, so this meant I would have to catch the last train from Carlisle, so I would be back home 3 hours later than scheduled. Just as I was about to go back into the village and kill an hour in the pub a bus pulled into the car park. I asked the driver if he was a train replacement and he confirmed he was going to Carlisle. The coach didn't go straight to Carlisle, instead it stopped at all the train stations on route, so we arriving at the border town ten minutes after the departure of the 1941 service. So, this meant the dreaded drunken fuelled last train back home to Newcastle.

To cut this long (journey home) story short, I got wind of a bloke also travelling back to Newcastle who had been on the same replacement bus from Kilmarnock. He was kicking off big style in the station office about this shoddy service and demanded a taxi home. I casually strolled into the office and with my very best little boy look entreated for a share of the taxi ride, which the gentleman in question agreed to with the train station guard only too willing to help.

So, my return journey from a terrific day in Auchinleck was by coach and a taxi, arriving in Newcastle at 9.30pm then back home for ten. Of course, these transport shenanigans are all part of a football traveller's life, and I can live with the odd hiccup now and then, if the destination has been well worth the effort and today it certainly was.

Matchday Stats

Saturday 18th April 2015(2.30pm ko)

Scottish Junior Cup Semi-final 2nd leg

Auchinleck Talbot 2(Young 59 Milliken 71)

Hurlford United 1 (Robertson 51)

(5-2 on aggregate)

Att.1,700apx

Ground no.451

10. Satellite City

Glenrothes - Warout Stadium (May 2015)

Warout Stadium - a lovely mix of the brutalist and the verda (set off by a soupcon of blaze) Not my own metrical words, but a tweet I received from 100 Football Ground Club member Alex Anderson, when I announced that Glenrothes was the next stop on my Scottish tour.

Glenrothes formed part of the New Towns Act of 1946, which allowed the government to designate areas as new towns, basically set up to consider how best to repair and rebuild urban communities in the aftermath of World War II. Glenrothes was the second such town in Scotland, designated in 1948, following on from East Kilbride the year before. The town is in the heart of Fife, situated approximately 30 miles in between the cities of Edinburgh and Dundee. The name Glenrothes comes from its historical link with the Earl of Rothes, who owned much of the land with "Glen" (Scottish for valley) added to the name as it lies in the valley of the River Leven. The small village became one of the new towns, with the original plan to provide houses for miners at the newly established Rothes Colliery. The town now has a population of almost 30,000, having developed as an important industrial centre in Scotland's Silicon Glen sector from the early 1960's, with several major electronics and hi-tech companies setting up facilities in the town. Glenrothes is the administrative capital of Fife and has a quite unique town centre, as the majority is indoors within the Kingdom Shopping Centre, the largest of its kind in Fife.

My train from Newcastle arrived in Edinburgh at 9.25, and after a hearty breakfast and a patrol around the city record stores, I met up with Mark Wilkins at Waverley Station who was due to arrive up from London at 11.30. Mark is also a postman and has been delivering the post even longer than I have, having clocked up 30 years at Royal Mail. He also out trumps me with his football grounds total, when I asked what number Warout Stadium is, he said it was in the two thousand, one hundred and sixties!

This whole Matchday was made possible by the generosity of James Little who picked us up at the station and drove us over the Forth into Fife. On route, we stopped off in Kirkcaldy to visit the Robert Nairn Weatherspoon's pub (we didn't have time for a bevvy here when me and James went to Raith Rovers a few seasons ago) When we arrived in Glenrothes, it was just as I imagined it would be, with shitloads of roundabouts and one way systems, like Washington, which is just down the road from me, designated as a new town in 1964.

When we finally worked out the route to the Golden Acorn, we just had time for the one drink before heading to the ground. The Glens originally played at Dovecote Park where a record crowd of 5,400 attended the 6th Round Scottish Junior Cup tie against Shotts Bon Accord in 1968. The club moved just a half a mile south to the Warout Stadium in 1974 which has a capacity of 5,000, dominated by the main stand with the rest of the ground having grass banking which is beautifully maintained, with the large pitch separated by a surrounding oval track. The highest attendance recorded at the Warout Stadium is 5,600 for a 6th round Junior Cup tie with Cambuslang Rangers in 1974.

When we arrived inside we were greeted by John Hay the club's media man,

"You must be Shaunee" he said, as he was expecting me to be at the game after I had announced my destination on Twitter earlier in the week. He introduced us to the club chairman Dougie Cooper, who didn't just shake my hand, he crushed it, so like a big soft shite I said

"Please to meet you ... ow!"

The chairman invited us into the boardroom at half time for tea and sandwiches, so yet again more splendid hospitality which was gratefully received by myself and my fellow travel companions.

The committee room is filled with club memorabilia and a huge collection of pennants from the teams the club has faced throughout their history. Glenrothes Football Club were formed in 1964 and enjoyed instant success by winning the Fife County League in their second competitive season, the first of three successive league titles. The Fife Regional League was won in 1969-70 and they were crowned champions on four occasions through the seventies and twice in the eighties, the last of which was in 1984-85. Since the Fife clubs became part of the East Region Junior set up, they were relegated from the Super League in 2006, but made a quick return after clinching the Premier League the following season.

Exactly four years from the day the club was founded, they reached the final of the Junior Cup. They negotiated some tricky ties on route to the final at Hampden Park, where they met Johnstone Burgh in front of a crowd of 28,800 at Hampden Park. The match finished 2-2, but three days later the clubs returned to Hampden for the replay, with the Glens narrowly losing out in a 4-3 thriller, witnessed by an audience of 21,700.

The club have won an array of cup honours over the last half a decade but the Junior Cup took pride of place in 1974-75. The club defeated Arbroath Victoria, Dunipace, St Roch's, Cumbernauld United, Baillieston after a replay and Ashfield in the semi-final. Hampden Park again hosted the final where they faced Rutherglen Glencairn in front of a 17,776 crowd, who witnessed the Glens Willie Cunningham grab the only goal of the game to take the prestigious trophy to the Warout Stadium for the only time in their proud history.

The season 74-75 wasn't just a big season for the Glen, or indeed a 1995 Top 20 hit for The Connells, it was also my first proper season of regularly attending matches. My Dad took me to Newcastle's first two home games of the campaign, a 3-2 win over Coventry City, then on the following Wednesday a 2-2 draw with Sheffield United, my first match under the floodlights. The games during this season hold my fondest football memories, maybe because my time of going to the match with my Dad was brief, as he was one of many Newcastle fans that vowed never to return to St James Park when the club sold Malcolm MacDonald to Arsenal in 1976. Highlights of my first season include beating reigning champions Leeds United 3-0 just before Christmas and "Supermac" scoring a late goal in a 3-1 over Arsenal, a week after he scored all five goals for England against Cyprus at Wembley.

Another match from this season that I must mention was the debut of Alfie Conn for Tottenham Hotspur, the Kirkcaldy born forward having just moved to London from Rangers. Conn scored three first half goals with Spurs leading 4-0 at the break, becoming the first Scottish player to mark a first appearance in England by scoring a hat-trick. He is the son of the Alfie Conn senior, who was one of the famous 'Terrible Trio' that played for Hearts in the 1950s. He left Spurs for Celtic in 1977, becoming the first post-World War Two player to play for both old firm clubs. For the record, Newcastle were brilliant in the second half, but Conn had done the damage in the first 45 and the final score was 2-5.

Glenrothes were up against Forfar West End, with both clubs going into this game level on 32 points, but with the hosts having played more games they still had an outside chance of being relegated.

The match was a basic game of two halves with the Glenrothes having the better of the opening period before taking the lead just before half time, when John Martin was put clear and finished with a neat nutmeg through the goalkeeper's legs. After the restart, West End were on the front foot and equalised after just three minutes when a long throw in fell into the path of Matty Reynolds who found the net from six yards.

The Glens poor start to the second half continued, being reduced to 10 men after the number eight was shown a straight red card. Both teams had chances to win the game but the match finished with the clubs still remaining level on points at the bottom section of the East Region Premier League. This was Glenrothes last league game of the season and the final 33 points total wasn't enough. Forfar West End won their last two fixtures, while Bathgate Thistle bagged four more points to leapfrog the Glens and relegate them into the North Division.

After the game, we heading back to Edinburgh, listening to the football scores coming through on the car radio which had me really pished off by another pitiful performance from NUFC, losing to already doomed Queens Park Rangers which meant us Geordies had to sweat it out for another week, as the threat of relegation went to the last weekend of the season.

We completed a Weatherspoon's hat-trick, calling at The White Lady, another uncharted JDW next to Edinburgh Zoo in Corstorphine, before James dropped us off at Waverley at 6pm. Me and Mark were both booked on the 1830, so there was time for a few swift ones in the Jingling Geordie before running across the road for our train.

Another terrific day in great company, hopefully Mark will be joining me again in this odyssey while James is a crucial part of this story, so I'll defo be seeing him again next season.

Matchday Stats

Saturday 16th May 2015

East Region Premier League

Glenrothes 1(Martin 40) Forfar West End (Reynolds 48)

Att.170.est

Ground no. 462

11. Life is a Motorway

Pollok - Newlandsfield Park

My target of half a dozen grounds ticked off this season looked to have falling one short, as I expected Glenrothes and the Junior Cup Final my last two trips north this season. Just when I was beginning to think my football season was finally over, along comes another invitation to a game, as I joined my north-east based Groundhopping friends Katie Wallace and Lee Stewart for our third road trip to the west of Scotland in the space of a week. The previous Wednesday we heading across the A69 then up the A74 to Wishaw Juniors, another former Junior Cup winner, but as they lifted the trophy back in 1888, that's a wee bit too early to qualify for a chapter in this book.

On Sunday, we were in Kilmarnock for the final of the Junior Cup, where Auchinleck Talbot captured the biggest cup prize in Scotland for the eleventh time with a 2-1 win over Musselburgh Athletic. The Bot were soon back in cup action again with a semi-final tie in the Evening Times Champions Cup at Pollok, a club I've been really looking forward to visiting (must be the black 'n' white stripes...Ed) as part of this project, so after getting picked up later than originally planned, we crossed the Tyne Bridge at four o'clock for yet another six-hour round road trip.

Pollok FC formed back in 1908 and had their first successful period during the Second World War years, winning the Glasgow Junior Cup and the Glasgow Dryburgh Cup in 1941-42. They won more honours during this decade and reached the semi-finals of the Junior Cup in 1944-45. In the quarter-final they beat Fauldhouse United after a protest, winning 3-1 in the replay in front of a crowd of over 15,000 at Newlandsfield. Many spectators had to leave the ground as they were unable to see any of the match action, so they headed to the Pollokshaws East Station just 50 yards away, where for the price of a platform ticket they had a bird's eye view of the game. In the semi-finals, they lost out to eventual winners Burnbank Athletic 1-0 before a crowd of 25,000 with the ground full signs going up an hour before kick-off.

The club benefitted after the demise of senior club Third Lanark in 1967, with many fans switching their allegiance to their south side neighbours. The club won the Central League Cup the first time in 1978 and lifted the trophy on eight further occasions, the same number of times they won the Central Division from their first title success in 1978-79.

The Scottish Junior Cup first took residence at Newlands in 1981, beating Arthurlie in front of a crowd of over 13,000 at Hampden Park with Norrie Fulton grabbing the decisive goal. Pollok followed up this success in 1985, returning to Hampden to beat Petershill 3-1 in the replay after a 1-1 draw, but missed out on the double the following season, losing 3-2 to Auchinleck Talbot in the centenary final.

The 1990's was a hugely successful period for the 'Lok including a third Junior Cup triumph in 1997, defeating Tayport 3-1 in the final at Motherwell's Fir Park. However, disappointment followed 12 months later as Arthurlie finally gained revenge for that '81 defeat by gubbing Pollok 4-0 at Fir Park.

Following the reconstructing of the Junior Leagues in 2002, Pollok were placed in the West Region Super League Premier Division. The 'Lok were the first club to win the division and have been champions in 2004-05, 2006-07 and 2007-08, making them the division's most successful club. Those last two triumphs coincided with the SFA inviting the winners of the 3 major Junior leagues and the Junior Cup winners to take part in the Senior Scottish Cup. Pollok overcame St Cuthbert Wanderers and faced Montrose in the 2nd round, achieving a 2–2 draw at Links Park, but narrowly losing the replay at Newlandsfield, then the following year they were knocked out by Spartans FC in the 1st round.

Pollok were relegated for the first time following a disastrous 2013-14 season, having four different managers and the club also entangled with off the field problems. This season under the guidance of Tony McInally they've comfortably won the league, so they'll be back in the West Region's top division next season.

Throughout my many years of travelling to football I surely must been on every 'A' road in England. My first experience of a long stretch of motorway was in 1976, when me and my day travelled to Wembley and then Old Trafford the following year. In those days, it was at least a good six-hour drive to that there London and I travelled south on many occasions to watch United on the Supporters Club coaches during the 1980's and 90's. My oldest friend Ian Patrick drove me and his son Lee to Plymouth and back in a day for an FA Cup 3rd round tie in 2010, but the daftest long journey the three of us did was all the way to the other St James Park. Newcastle played a Testimonial game at Exeter City on a Tuesday night and

Ian drove us there and straight back just so we could tick off the ground.

I've travelled to quite a few matches over this past season with Katie and Lee. Katie purchased a car early in the season and the grounds total of the groundhopping couple has rising dramatically, after having to usually rely on public transport for their football fix. Lee joined the *100 Football Grounds Club* in May 2009 and first met at a game at Darlington Cleveland Bridge the following year. I recognised Lee as he was wearing a Plymouth Argyle jersey, the team he supports after living in Devon for five years, during which time he saw The Pilgrims win two league titles and so became instantly hooked. Lee returned to Peterlee in the summer of 2004, his hometown is found in between Sunderland and Hartlepool in County Durham.

Lee met Katie in September 2010 when he was the DJ at the Highfield Hotel near her home in Houghton-le-Spring. The hotel was hosting a singles night so Katie went along with a friend for a laugh, where she didn't find an appropriate Innamorato but still managed to score! With a name like Katie Wallace you'd imagine she'd be a Scottish lassie, well she was born in Hamilton, but not the town in South Lanarkshire, but the other one, found on the north island of New Zealand. Katie's father emigrated from the north-east and met the woman which turned out to be Katie's mother, so after living most of her life in the Waikato and the Bay of Plenty areas, she thought she would try her luck in England in November 2002. She bought a one-way ticket and originally stayed with relatives and hasn't looked back, content enough to have swapped sunny skies for grey days in the north-east.

Since they've been together Lee has got Katie into proper football, managing to successfully get her away from regularly watching Sunderland (which is her Dad's team) onto non-league football and groundhopping, so much so that she's developed a touch of our OCD, wanting to complete leagues and over the last year my influence has rubbed off on them as they have both became Weatherspoon's enthusiasts.

The late start and the heavy traffic meant we didn't pull into the Morrisons car park outside the ground until 7pm. Although we missed out on our usual Weatherspoon's tea, I wasn't going to be denied another tick so I ran along to the Sir John Stirling Maxwell by myself for a swift pint, while Lee and Katie went straight into the ground.

Pollok are based in Newlands in the south side of Glasgow, located less than 2 miles south of the River Clyde. The district originated as farmland around the Newlands manor house and developed as an upmarket area of Victorian houses with large gardens. The White Cart Water splits Newlands from Shawlands, the area consisting mostly of tenement flats and is surrounded by the neighbouring districts of Crossmyloof, Langside and Pollokshaws. The nearby Queen's Park was developed in the late 19th century in response to the increasing population on the south side of the Clyde, with the need for open spaces within the large community. The park was opened in 1857, designed by Sir Joseph Paxton and dedicated to the memory of Mary, Queen of Scots - who lost the Battle of Langside near the park.

When I arrived back at Newlandsfield Park quite a big crowd had gathered outside the paying entrance with a large following from Auchinleck. When I entered the ground, I was taking aback by its splendour. Although it's basically four sides of terraces it's a gem, dominated by a 1,500 capacity covered enclosure on one side. The roof is decked out in black and white with the club and ground name proudly displayed in the centre. The dugouts are in front of the stand and opposite there's now a row of apartments to block the view from the train station. The Southsides local team began life at Haggs Park in the Pollok Estate, but were forced into a move during the 1926-27 season when the city council wanted the land for school pitches, despite the club spending hundreds of pounds on improving the facilities. After playing temporarily at Rosebery Park and the Queen Mary Tea Gardens in Thornliebank they acquired Newlandsfield Park in 1928.

The Champions Cup is an end of season mini cup competition for the five winners of the West Region leagues. Talbot were looking for a hat-trick of wins in this competition and another trophy in what's been a terrific season for the Bot. They took the lead after quarter of an hour when following on from his magnificent strike in the Junior Cup final, Dwayne Hyslop scored with a much simpler task to fire in a right-wing cross from twelve yards. At the interval, I expected the Super Premier champions to march into the final but the 'Lok had other ideas in what was a cracking second half.

After the restart, Tam Hanlon equalised from the penalty spot with ten minutes gone, following a handball, then moments later their job was made easier when Bot defender Derek McCulloch totally lost his rag. He was shown a red card after pushing over an opposing player, before arguing the toss with fellow players and the referee, then to top it all off on his way to the dressing room he chinned the corner flag!

Pollok instantly took advantage of the extra man when Robbie Winters was on hand to head home a right-wing cross from close range to make it 2-1 on 57 minutes. This is the same Robbie Winters who played for Dundee United and Aberdeen during the 1990's. The forty-year-old went onto play for a host of clubs throughout Scotland, Norway, Iceland and one appearance for both Scotland and ... Luton Town.

It was Gordon Pope who scored the decisive winning goal in Sunday's final with a coolly taken penalty, but he was denied from 12 yards this time 'round as Jordan Longmuir pulled off a fine save in the 67th minute. Talbot pressed for an equaliser and were rewarded a few minutes later when a free kick from a central position found Graham Wilson, who showed good control to pick the ball out of the air and finish neatly from ten yards.

Auchinleck should've had the tie wrapped up late on but were denied by some stunning saves from Longmuir who took the match into a penalty shootout after keeping the score locked at two apiece. After a man of the match performance from the Pollok 'keeper I fully expected him to again produce something special and he didn't let me down. Talbot's first penalty smacked the crossbar before the 'Lok number 1 pulled off two good saves to book his team a place in the final with a 3-2 penalty shootout victory.

Pollok hosted the final the following Saturday and faced Blantyre Victoria, and the ever-reliable Winters was again on the mark with his young'un David Winters bagging a brace in a 3-1 win to complete a league and champions cup double for the Southsides local team.

I was back home much later than normal, Katie pulling outside my house just before 1am, so there was just time for just 4 hours sleep before heading off to graft next morning. I'll quite happily sacrifice that much needed extra kip for what turned out to be one of my favourite grounds out of the 67 I've visited this season. Not only was it a cracking venue but the match was entertaining too and a good one to finish the season on. All in all, this means I can now finally make it official, after 116 matches and 447 goals, I'm now declaring the brilliant football season of 2014-15 officially over.

Matchday Stats

Wednesday 10th June 2015 (7.30pm ko)

Evening Times Champions Cup semi-final

Pollok 2(Hanlon 54pen Winters 57)

Auchinleck Talbot 2(Hyslop 16 Wilson 70)

(Pollok win 3-2 on penalties)

Att.800.est

Ground no.465

12. Blue Desire

Kilsyth Rangers - Duncansfield Park (July 2015)

This was the week of the big "Whey-aye Five-O" so I booked some holiday time to celebrate leaving my forties and chalking up a half a century of cheating death. After much thought, I decided to go somewhere different to celebrate the occasion and as I'm not the sort of person who gives into cliché or type, there was no trip to New York or an exotic holiday in the sun.

After much debate, I decided to head as far north as possible, so a night on the ale in Inverness and an afternoon visiting to the northernmost senior league ground in the UK. I obviously couldn't head over the border without savouring some Scottish Joons action, so I took off on the Wednesday afternoon, booking a guest house in Glasgow. A few nights off the leash in the big city, meant I could check out a few pubs, do some vinyl shopping and bag a couple of grounds off the list. The midweek pre-season friendly fixtures worked out perfectly presenting me with consecutive nights which formed a Kil' Rangers double.

I left Newcastle at lunch time and on arrival in Edinburgh I caught the bus onwards to Glasgow. That's because it only cost a quid on the bus, yes just 100 British pence if you book on the Megabus website. I arrived at 4pm, checked into the guest house which was just behind Sauchiehall Street, so it was handy for The Hengler's Circus 'Spoons, where I supped a quick couple of pints before catching the 89 bus from Buchanan Street to Kilsyth.

When I asked the bus driver for a return ticket to Kilsyth I realised it was yet another Scottish town that I had pronounced incorrectly. I requested a journey to Kil-sith when it's obviously Kil-syth, as in Bruce For-syth, it's obvious really, the clue was in the spelling. After finally establishing where I wanted to go with the bus driver I handed him a five spot for my return journey.

The town is a narrow strip of land about 200 feet above sea level, between the Kilsyth Hills and the River Kelvin. The town occupies a sheltered position in the Kelvin Valley, between Kirkintilloch to the west and Falkirk in the east, with the "Tak Ma Doon Road" from Stirling heading from the north to Cumbernauld in the south. The North Lanarkshire town has always been one of the main routes between Glasgow, Falkirk and Edinburgh, and is very close to the Roman Antonine Wall, and the Forth & Clyde Canal.

There is archaeological evidence of a settlement since Neolithic times, before The Romans got in on the act building forts, including the Antonine Wall fortresses of Bar Hill and Croy Hill which are clearly still visible from the town. In the Middle Ages its central narrow location made it the prime site for two castles at Balcastle and Colzium which have since been destroyed.

The Civil War Battle of Kilsyth took place on hillsides between Kilsyth and Banton, as part of the Wars of the Three Kingdoms in August 1645. This was a series of civil wars fought in England, Scotland and Ireland between the Royalists, who supported Charles I against the Covenanters who had controlled Scotland since 1639 and supported the English Parliament, the battle was another victory for the Royalist general 1st Marquess of Montrose over the Covenanters, despite a numerical disadvantage and marked the end of William Baillie's pursuit of the Royalist forces.

Modern day Kilsyth has a population of just over 10,000 and is now more a commuter town to nearby Glasgow, having a high proportion of council housing, built during the 1950's replacing old miner's rows and run down accommodation. The town can also claim to be the birthplace of the winter sport of curling. The Kilsyth Curling Club was formed in 1716 and is the oldest surviving club in the world. The sport has been played in Kilsyth since the 16th century on the Curling Pond in the Colzium Estate in the east of the town.

The bus to North Lanarkshire took a good 50 minutes, but the bus stop as it turned out is just outside the ground. I knew I had arrived at the correct stop because of my sixth sense, my in-built football ground antenna. In the days before satellite navigation or Google maps, it was a case of travelling to the destination town or city then asking someone wearing the club colours where the ground is. Most of the time though bothering a member of the public wasn't required as I would suddenly get this inner compass sensation which sends a message to my brain and diverts my eyes in the direction of a set of floodlight pylons.

Duncansfield is another belter Junior ground, dominated by the pitch length covered terrace enclosure on the far side. The stand has a con-iron peaked roof with an old advert in large capital letters for Whiteinch Demolition Ltd, with room for 500 spectators. Opposite at the entrance side is terracing with grass banking behind each goal, with a perimeter track around the pitch. The main area of the ground has a car park and two separate buildings; the members bar and the changing rooms. A great feature of the ground is its proper players tunnel, which leads from the changing rooms, then underneath the terrace and onto the pitch between the dugouts. The current capacity is set at 2,000 but the record attendance at Duncansfield Park is 8,740 for a Scottish Junior cup tie against Broxburn Athletic in 1951

When I arrived, I was approached by Russell from the club committee who took me inside the Members Club and made sure I got a cuppa tea and sorted out a pin badges, courtesy of fellow committeeman John. I had a chat with some of the Kilsyth fans in the bar, who told me of past glories and players, all good crack and very hospitable.

Nicknamed "The Wee Gers" Kilsyth Rangers formed in 1913 and have won the Junior Cup on two occasions. The first of which was in 1955 against Duntocher Hibs, when a huge Hampden Park crowd of 64,976 saw the game end in a 1–1 draw. Less than half that figure saw Kilsyth win the replay 4–1 with all four goals scored by Alex Querrie, the club's most prolific striker, who is the only player to achieve this feat in a final (so far)

The Wee Gers were red hot favourites to win the trophy two years later but narrowly lost the 1957 final 1-0 against Banks O'Dee. It was ten years before Rangers again graced the final, winning at the second attempt beating Rutherglen Glencairn 3–1 after a 1–1 draw in the first game at Hampden, which was played in front of 22,000 fans.

The club have won a large selection of cup honours, especially during the 1950's when they lifted the Stirlingshire Junior Cup eight years running and were twice Central League Champions during that decade. Recent years have brought league and cup success for the first time in a long while. After a gap of 30 years the club won the Central League Division One title in 2002-03 followed by the Superleague First Division title in 2004–05.

The club has been a decent breeding ground for players who have gone onto senior level, including six players who have gone on to win full Scotland caps, such as: James Dougall (1 cap 1932), George Mulhall (3 caps 1960-64), Drew Jarvie (3 caps 1971), David Stewart (1cap 1977), Frank McGarvey (7 caps 1979-84) and Willie Wallace (7 caps 1965-69).

The Wee Gers were in pre-season action for the first time this season against St Roch's. Before the match, I was outside the changing rooms and I overheard one of the team managers telling his team, that this ISN'T a pre-season friendly and to treat it as a competitive match. Judging by the performance and result I'm guessing I had earwigged on the away dressing room.

Kilsyth donning a red changed kit fielded an inexperienced side and were punished for some sloppy play. They fell a goal behind when a cross was cut out by the defender who headed past his own 'keeper after quarter of an hour. Just before the break Jordan Logan banged in a brace, the first with a mazy run and good finish, before finding the bottom right hand corner again after good work from Mussa. The big number 19 for St Roch's looked a good player, his stance and movement reminded me of Mario Balotelli, but thankfully he has a good attitude and no stupid haircut. It was he, Baboucarr Mussa who made it 4-0 ten minutes from the restart with a close-range finish, before being subbed along with his strike partner Logan.

Kilsyth played much better after the fourth goal, after rearranging the back-four and adding a bit more width they looked much better going forward, but were unable to find the net and the visitors comfortably kept the clean sheet in a good pre-season performance.

After the match, I made sure I caught the last bus back to Glasgow, arriving at the bus stop with plenty of time to give the breadknife a ring to let her know I was still alive. Before heading back to my digs I stopped off at the Bon Accord on North Street for a nightcap, which was recommended by a few comments on Facebook. Overall a great first day in Glasgow and another to look forward to when I'll be heading to North Ayrshire for the second part of my Kil' Rangers double at Kilwinning.

Matchday Stats

Wednesday 22nd July 2015 (7pm ko)

Pre-season friendly

Kilsyth Rangers 0

St Roch's 4(Heenak 15OG Logan 40,41 Mussa 55)

Att.102hc

Ground no.472

13. Happy Birthday!

Kilwinning Rangers - Abbey Park (July 2015)

The second of my Kil' Rangers double as part of my
Glasgow stopover, was 20 miles south of the city in
Kilwinning. After having a basic breakfast at the guest
house, being one of each item on a plate the next size up
from a saucer, I was ready for a good look around Glasgow
and a few pubs, which included catching a local train to
Anniesland to tick off another Wetherspoon establishment.
My digs were on Renfrew Street which was in a good city
location, although the place itself was a bit of a flea pit, but
I can't complain too much, considering how much it cost.
The bed was comfortable enough, the Wi-Fi signal was
excellent, but it wasn't a room with a view, facing a brick
wall of the neighbouring building, the window kept open
with a small shampoo bottle as the latch was broken.

After a pleasant day in Glasgow, I caught the train down to
Kilwinkie at 6pm. I didn't have time for a drink in the town
before or after the game, but a steady pub crawl of about 5
pubs from station to ground is an option for visitors. The
town lies on the River Garnock, known as "The Crossroads
of Ayrshire" Its ancient name is Segdoune/Saigtow from
the word 'Sanctoun', meaning 'Saint town'. Kilwinning is
steeped in religious history deriving from its 12th century
Abbey, the site of which is said to have been revealed to
Saint Winning by a visionary Angel. It was founded
sometime between 1162 and 1188 with monks coming from
Kelso, dedicated to Saint Winning and the Virgin Mary.
The date assigned to St Winin is 715 AD, when his festival

was celebrated on the 21st January, when a town fair was held and called St Winning's Day.

According to legend the Saint sent his monks to fish in the River Garnock, however no matter how hard they tried they could even catch a tiddler. The dejected saint placed a curse on the river, preventing it from ever having fish in its waters; the river responded by changing course and thereby avoiding the curse.

This part of North Ayrshire was where the missionary enterprise began in Scotland, with the Celtic Christians or Culdees founded here. The town is also home to the oldest Masonic Lodge not only in Scotland, but in the world. The Mother Lodge of Scotland attributing its origins to the 12th Century, and is often called Mother Kilwinning

Kilwinning was a noted centre of Archery in medieval times. Later the town had an association with coal mining, quarrying, iron-founding and textile manufacture, with the Pringle knitwear company originally manufactured their goods in the town.

The town fell within the area designated to Irvine New in 1966, expanding with new estates built on surrounding farmland to meet the planned increase in population. This included new inhabitants relocated from the Glasgow overflow and according to the last Census the population is just under 16,000.

Modern industries include the manufacture of plastics and electronics. The refurbishment of Kilwinning Main Street in 2010 by Irvine Bay Regeneration Company led to several new businesses opening shops in the town centre, one of a number of regeneration projects in the Irvine Bay area.

As for the town's football club, they formed in 1899 and are affectionately known as "The Buffs" a nickname giving to them by the Irvine Herald newspaper after an emphatic win over Kilmarnock Belgrove in 1900. Kilwinning Rangers began life as a juvenile club, originally playing at Blacklands Park, which they shared with senior team Eglinton Seniors, before officially joining the Junior ranks on the 26th July 1902. The club bagged their first trophy in the Ayrshire Cup in 1905 and won the Ayrshire First Division in 1920-21, becoming champions an additional nine times throughout their history.

The Junior Cup was won for the first time in 1909, beating Strathclyde 1-0 in a replay after the original tie finished goalless. The Buffs lost out twice in the final against Ashfield in 1910 and St Roch's in 1922, before finally lifting the trophy again after a 90 year wait, when a goal from Gerry Peline was good enough to beat Kelty Hearts at Firhill Park. That 1999 success meant they were the first and last Ayrshire club to win the Scottish Junior Cup in the 20th century, which topped off their greatest season when they won six trophies in 1998-99.

Kilwinning were the second club and the first from Ayrshire to win the West Super League in the 2003-04 season, but over recent years they've yo-yoed between the Super League First Division and the Ayrshire District League, winning promotion again last season.

Abbey Park is hidden off Church Street, just a short walk from Main Street. I noticed a couple of elderly gentleman, one wearing a blue scarf who I followed down the street into the ground. From the corner entrance, there's seven wooden sleeper steps running up half way towards the away dugout. These sleepers are also behind the far goal with a covered terraced enclosure opposite. The main part of the ground is down one side behind the home dugout. There's cabins which provides catering, a hospitality bar, toilets and the changing rooms. After walking around the ground I discovered there's another paying entrance around the far side, although this too gives no clue that this is actually the home of Kilwinning Rangers. Apart from the lack of signage the ground looks in great nick, the pitch is immaculate (aye, I know it was still July) and overall the lawns and facilities are well maintained.

Kilmarnock are regular pre-season visitors to Abbey Park. The Buffs wear blue and white hooped shirts, but tonight they were kitted out in an all lemon number, while Killie wore all orange, so this along with the bright sunshine gave it a taste of summer fruits.

Kilwinning took the lead after just seven minutes when a 20-yard free kick from a central position was nicely placed out of the 'keeper's reach by Ben Lewis. Kilmarnock quickly responded and equalised minutes later when Scott McClean headed home a left-wing cross. The first half was pretty even, but it was the senior side that dominated the second half, snatching victory with two goals in the last ten minutes. The game seemed to be heading for a draw until substitute Jack Whittaker got on the end of a right-wing cross with a neat side foot volley at the far post. Moments later a shot from Adam Frizzell took a big reflection off the defender to wrong foot the goalie to make it 3-1. I asked a couple of Kilmarnock supporters who scored the goals and they were only too willing to help. As it turned out they had made a mistake, so one of the fans came looking for me to give me the right information. He was relieved to have found me, it was as if he wouldn't have been able to sleep that night knowing he had conversed the wrong information to that lonely traveller from down south. For a friendly it was a decent game and judging by this performance I think the Buffs will do OK in the Super League First Division this season, while Killie have a few talented young'uns on their books.

After returning to Glasgow I called for a few bevvies in the Horse Shoe Bar, then on to Sauchiehall Street, before retiring back at my digs after a long eventful day. I had a smashing couple of days in Glasgow, leaving the city on the Megabus back to Edinburgh the following afternoon. I met Debra at Waverley as she was arriving on the 1555 train from Newcastle, from there we headed to the James Little guest house for our overnight stay. There were mince 'n' tatties on the teatime menu which was good blotting paper for our pub crawl around the south side of Edinburgh. We were joined by James' pal John and later Jamie McQueen, who had been to the match at Whitehill Welfare for what was a cracking night out at some smashing real ale pubs.

After a heavy drink and a late night, me and the breadknife were up sharp at 7am for the Megabus trip to Inverness, where we arrived just after midday. As my birthday fell on a Saturday there had to be football involved, so on our arrival there was just enough time to drop off our luggage at the hotel, buy our tickets and catch the 1247 Aberdeen train to Elgin for City v Stirling Albion.

Before the match there was the obvious stop off at Weatherspoon's, where I enjoyed a tasty Highland Burger and my first birthday drinks of the day. Just prior to kick off I had a quick flick through the matchday programme to find that Elgin City were good enough to wish me a happy 50th birthday, which was a very nice touch ... but how on Earth did they know?

Another canny bevvy was enjoyed for my birthday night in Inverness where we found some cracking little pubs and a few lively ones. The town centre was jumping and I've never seen so many lasses wearing mini-skirts. So much so that I saw more pairs of legs in one night than I've seen watching football so far this season.

So, that was my "Whey-aye-five-o" birthday... a wee tour of Scotland, 3 matches and 4 days on the lash. I can now sadly boast my half a century birthday was spent at the most northerly senior league ground in Britain and not many people, if at all anyone outside Elgin, can make that claim.

Matchday Stats

Thursday 23rd July 2015

Pre-Season Friendly

Kilwinning Rangers 1 (Lewis 7)

Kilmarnock XI 3 (McClean 13 Whittaker 80 Frizzell 81)

Att.270.est

Ground no.473

14. Saturday Superhouse

Renfrew - New Western Park (August 2015)

As part of this continuous journey I was hoping to tick off Renfrew on the day they moved into their new home, as Groundhoppers love a first or last game at a ground. I booked advance train tickets for the start of the new season and it worked out perfectly, as the club announced the opening of New Western Park would be against their former landlords Johnstone Burgh in the group stage of the League Cup.

I caught the direct train from Newcastle to Glasgow, where on arrival I stopped off for breakfast and numerous cups of coffee at the Camperdown Place. I've been to Glasgow so much over the last year that my daughter's friends thought I was having an affair. They were concerned about Laura's parents, thinking her dad was knocking off some Scottish boiler!

I arranged to meet up with James Little at Buchanan Street Bus Station at 11am, to catch the X23 bus for the five-mile journey west of the city to Renfrew. We originally planned to get the train to Yoker, then catch the ferry across the river. Because of its proximity to the south bank of the River Clyde, a ferry has operated between Renfrew and Yoker on the opposite bank for more than 300 years. The last car ferry was retired in 1984, but a frequent passenger-only ferry still plies the route, but we decided to bus it to save us a bit time and gain extra pub minutes.

On route to the match we stopped off at the Braehead shopping complex, found just off the M8 motorway, which was opened not far from the town centre in 1999. I wasn't there to do a spot of shopping mind, there was a Weatherspoon's tick to be had amongst its many bars, restaurants and attractions. As someone who earns his pennies by walking around the largest shopping centre in the UK, five days a week, 46 weeks a year, this felt like a home from home. After walking amongst the herd of sad Saturday shoppers (Saturdays are for football not shopping) we finally located The Lord of the Isles pub. We have a few swift pints before making more use of our £3.80 all day ticket to catch the bus to the town centre. The bus stopped outside the eye-catching town hall which dominates the skyline. The building is a mix of French and Gothic styles, featuring its square tower standing 105 feet high with corbelled turrets at each corner and was designed by James Lamb of Paisley.

Renfrew has a population of about 22,000 and is known as the "Cradle of the Royal Stewarts" due to its connection with the Royal house of Scotland and Great Britain. The town gained royal burgh status in 1397, becoming the county town of Renfrewshire and is also a barony. The current Baron of Renfrew is HRH Prince Charles. Down our way, he is known as The Prince of Wales, but up in this part of the world he's the Duke of Rothesay, who holds lands in the area as part of the principality of Scotland.

The best thing about Scotland is you never need to go too far to see a castle, however there is little evidence of the Royal Stewart castle which dates to the 12th century, built by Walter fitz Alan, High Steward of Scotland. The tactical location of this castle was to prevent the eastern expansion of the Somerled lordship and to bade off Norse invaders. It was rebuilt and extended in the 13th century by James Stewart and became the chief residence of Clan Stewart. During its history, it was captured by the English during the Wars of Scottish Independence and King Edward I of England gave a charter to Renfrew to Henry de Lacy, Earl of Lincoln in 1301. The castle was later back in Scottish hands when it was recaptured by The Stewarts with the help of Sir Colin Campbell of Lochow. The King of Scots resided in the castle for almost a century from 1390 in the reign of Robert III through to King James III in 1488. The castle eventually fell into decay and was converted into a soap works before being demolished in the 19th century.

The nearest pub to the bus stop is the Davidson bar, where we stayed for a couple of pints and watched a boring Premier League opening day fixture between Man Yoo and Spurs, before walking along to the ground. On the way, we passed the original Western Park which is nothing but barren land and no clues that this was once the proud home of Renfrew FC for over a century. The club were founded on the 6th May 1912, taking over Western Park from the defunct Junior Club Renfrew Victoria, who had called it a day and vacated the ground two years earlier. There was also a senior side which played in the town in the late 19th century, who took part in early years of the Scottish Cup. The club were successful from the off, winning the Scottish Junior Division One title twice and lifting the Renfrewshire Cup for the first time in 1917, a trophy they have gone on the win ten times. This was also the year when they reached their first Junior Cup final, navigating everyone round without conceding a goal and scoring 18 goals over the six ties, until the cup final replay saw St Mirren Juniors bag the only goal of the game to claim the top prize. It was a similar story in 1962, a single goal defeat to Rob Roy in the replay after a 1-1 draw, then in 2001 they completed a unique Junior Cup final hat-trick. The Frew faced Carnoustie Panmure at Firhill Park and played out yet another draw, however the days of replays are long gone, so after 120 goalless minutes they overcame their opponents 6-5 in a penalty shoot-out, with Neil Shearer scoring the decisive spot-kick.

The blue and white striped shirts of The Frew have won a host of local cup competition and in the league, they claimed the Central League Division One title in 1991-92. Their highest finish since the Juniors reconstruction was in 2005-06 when they finished runners-up to Auchinleck Talbot in the West Super League Premier Division.

The move to a new ground has been mooted for over 30 years and at long last the club begun a new era on the edge of Renfrew Retail Park. The ground has all the amenities in one large building behind the goal with a covered terrace on side. The ground has floodlights and a superb 3G pitch, which is good news for Groundhoppers during the winter months. The stadium is a working progress, so with more funding further improvements will be made, including the option to extend the stand.

Before the match kicked-off I got myself a coffee and some plotting paper to soak up the ale. I opted for a speciality pie, which was a bit pricier than your standard mince scabby-eye. Imagine my disappointment as I savoured my first morsel, to discover that is was just a standard chicken curry pie, so the "speciality" must have been the curry sauce.

It was quite fitting that Johnstone Burgh provided the opposition for the first match at this new venue, having been kind enough to allow The Frew to ground share at Keanie Park last season. As for the game, there was little action in the first half and as the match progressed it was looking more likely that I was about to record my first goalless game of the season. The first decent chance fell to Burgh after an hour, when an effort from Jason Hardie hit the underside of the crossbar and fortunately for Renfrew the ball bounced on the goal line, before being safely cleared.

Renfrew finally broke the deadlock on 74 minutes, when Marc McDaid found room on the right to pick out Alan Kinney in the box who slotted the ball home. The win was sealed in injury time when Scott Arthur timed his run to perfection to stay onside before rounding the 'keeper and running the ball into the net. So, a good start to Renfrew at New Western Park, a win, a clean sheet and a decent crowd in attendance.

After the game, we caught the ten past four bus back to Glasgow. When we arrived, there was enough time to call in the Horse Shoe bar before catching the train to Edinburgh. We got there just in time for the pending full time scores, delighted to discover that the Heed won and for James a win for the Jam Tarts, plus the bonus of opening day defeats for the teams we despise the most. The other football scores also went my way so there was the rarity of my football bet kopping, so all this as well as a good day out in Renfrew, completed a full house of what I would call a perfect Soccer Saturday.

Matchday Stats

Saturday 6th August 2015

Euroscot Section League Cup

Renfrew 2(Kinney 74 Arthur 90+2) Johnstone Burgh 0

Att.300.est   Ground no.48

15. The Drinking Eye

Johnstone Burgh - Keanie Park (September 2015)

My original plan for this afternoon was to tick off one of the East Region clubs, with top choice being Whitburn Juniors as a return to their own ground was imminent. After the release of the latest round of fixtures, it turned out to be the only option in the east from the remaining clubs on the list, that was until they announcing a few days before my trip that a return to Central Park is still on hold. This meant heading across to the west, with only two choices available from the 13 remaining clubs to visit. The best option was Johnstone Burgh so I booking further trains from Edinburgh, leaving Newcastle on the 0945 and travelled straight there, without any refreshment stops, so I arrived just over three hours after departure.

During my preparation, I discovered there's two pubs in the Good Beer Guide in Johnstone so I had a few bevvies in Callum's and Rennies before the 2 o'clock kick off. Well, that's what I thought I did. I found the Callum's pub at the beginning of the High Street and after enjoying a pint of Jaw 'Brew Drop' and a swift Strathaven 'Ginger Jock', I had a toddle along to Rennie's which I knew was at the bottom of Collier Street. When I got there, I was drawn to a blackboard outside the pub which declared Gents - no shirt, no service Ladies - no shirt, no charge, so obviously, I had to go in and see if any women had taken up this fabulous offer. Unfortunately, on this occasion no one had, however my main concern in the bar was there wasn't any hand pumps to be had, so I just had to settle for a pint of Caledonian Best. It wasn't until a few days later while looking through my pictures, that I noticed the name of the pub in the photo was called Collier's Bar. So, I hadn't been to Rennies at all, so I've missed out on another pub from the GBG.

This annual publication of the encyclopaedia of great boozers has been a constant companion of mine throughout my travelling years. There is usually around 4,500 pubs in the guide and I've met someone who nearly did the lot, falling just a dozen short of completing the full book. He even flew across to Guernsey from Jersey during the Channel Island games football tournament, quickly ticked the pubs then returned to Jersey on the same plane back. You won't be too surprised when I tell you this OCD pub ticker and keen ale drinker is a Scottish lad.

I've mentioned drinking quite a few times already in this book which may give you the impression that I'm a bit of a plonky. Well I do enjoy a good drink but I'm not exactly a beer monster. When I was younger, drinking was all about being out on the lash with you mates, getting blotto and supping enough warm beer to give you enough Dutch courage to chat up the lasses. Now that I'm older, much wiser and not out on the pull, drinking beer has become a hobby. Just as I love visiting uncharted football grounds, the same goes for unexplored pubs, especially old buildings with historic character. You're already aware of my JD Wetherspoon obsession, well there's more, as my OCD of ticking things off and making lists also extends to the beer I drink. In 2008 I began registering a list which is never ending, logging down every real ale that I consume with well over one thousand ales (and counting) marked in the ledger.

The Renfrewshire town of Johnstone lies 12 miles west of Glasgow city centre and just 3 miles from the neighbouring town of Paisley, found on the edge of the Greater Glasgow Urban Area. The town was a planned community created and designed by the local Laird, George Ludovic Houston who held an estate in the town - the 1560 built Z plan tower house known as the House of Easter Cochrane, which he renamed Johnstone Castle when he took possession in 1733. The town's early population was around 1,500, which included the local estate and rural hinterland. George Houston became 4th Laird of Johnstone in 1757 at the age of 14. During his 58 years as Laird, George extended Johnstone Castle, developed the extensive coal mines at nearby Quarrelton and opened lime works at Floor Craig. In 1781 he began selling land for housing near the Bridge of Johnstone, to plan the layout of a new town. Houston designed street plans, two mirroring civic squares: Houston Square and Ludovic Square and by 1794 the town had gained its current parish church.

Johnstone developed through its main industry of thread-making and cotton weaving, with mills powered by the Black Cart Water which runs to the north of the town. The community expanded in the 1930s with freshly built residential estates, which addressed the problem of population density in the historic area of the town. Nowadays it chiefly serves as a commuter town for Paisley and Glasgow, with a population of almost 16,000. Although much of Johnstone's heritage has now disappeared, the remains of Johnstone Castle have been restored and went on the property market as a four-bedroom house in 2014.

During the many years writing my blog I've researched hundreds of clubs, but the formation of Johnstone Burgh in 1956 is quite unique. The club emerged from a newspaper article in the "Johnstone & Linwood Gazette" after a journalist that had been ordered out of the newspaper's office by his gaffer with orders not to return until he had a story. The journalist stood on the corner of Johnstone's Rankine Street and proceeded to ask locals their thoughts about forming a new football club to replace the former Scottish League side Johnstone.

From the article a new Junior football club was born and The Burgh soon found success, winning the treble of Central League, the West of Scotland Cup and the Glasgow Dryburgh Cup in 1958-59. Under the leadership of Jimmy Blackburn, they won two league titles in the 1960s, as well as lifting the prestigious Junior Cup twice. In 1964 they beat Cambuslang Rangers 3-0 in a replay after a 1-1 draw, then four years later a second tie was again required, after a 2-2 draw they overcame Glenrothes 4-3 with Hugh Glishan grabbing the winner in extra time.

It wasn't until the turn of the millennium that the Burgh reached their third final and yet again the final finished in a draw. The club faced Whitburn with goals from Colin Lindsay and John McLay saw the match finish all square after extra time. Johnstone Burgh won on penalties in their semi-final at Love Street, but failed to repeat this success in the 2000 final, losing the penalty shootout by four goals to three.

The following season they won the Central League Premier Division and since the rejigging of the leagues, they were Central District Second Division champions in 2009-10. Last term they finished runners-up to Rossvale in the Second Division, so return to Central Division One after they were relegated in 2011.

One of their former players is a former Scottish international who lives just down to road from me. Frank McAvennie started his playing career in Juniors football, signed by the Burgh for a £500 fee in 1979 from local amateur side - the 200 Club in Kirkintilloch. While at the club he had a trial for Partick Thistle, making the briefest of appearances, coming on as a substitute only to be substituted off in the same game. He was told by manager and former "Lisbon Lion" Bertie Auld that he would never make a career in the game. The following year he signed for St. Mirren and the rest as they say is history, a playing career on both sides of the border and the playboy lifestyle of booze, drugs and Page 3 tarts. (Lucky get!)

After my bevvy in the wrong pub, I headed to the ground in good time for kick off. The club have been based at James Y. Keanie Park since their formation, named after the builder who donated the land on which the ground was built. There is a barrel roofed covered terrace at the far side which sits on the halfway line with grass banking behind both goals. At the paying entrance side, there's the main building which houses the changing rooms, toilets and the snack bar, with a wooden shelter on the grass verge, behind the dugouts.

For several years, there have been plans in place to relocate to a new ground at Thomas Shanks Memorial Park less than one mile away, built in conjunction with the local council. I don't know if this will ever come to fruition, but there must be a solution to the drainage problems, which makes Keanie Park prone to flooding resulting in regular postponements.

Johnstone faced table toppers Thorniewood United, who went into this game with maximum points from their first three fixtures. The Burgh wearing their traditional all red kit with white trimmings were under the cosh for most of the first half, with the visitors from Viewpark creating the better chances.

As the game progressed it was beginning to look likely that a solitary goal would settle the result. That golden opportunity fell to Jack Heron on 73 minutes, who latched onto a flicked header to find himself clear on goal, making no mistake to fire under the 'keeper and break the deadlock.

The hosts almost immediately blew the lead, when just two minutes later a reckless challenge just inside the penalty area gave the referee an easy decision to award a spot kick. The Thorniewood number 7 Lennon had been in the running for my top bloke of the match award, but his penalty was saved and the easier chance from the follow up was blasting over the bar and into the grass banking behind the goal.

The Burgh wrapped up the victory two minutes from time when a neat ball was threaded into the path of substitute Jason Hardie, who fired a first-time effort past the Wood 'keeper, then a minute later Thorniewood's miserable afternoon was complete when goalkeeper Cherrie was sent off for handball just outside the box. The win took Burgh level with Thorniewood as five clubs shared top spot after winning three of their first four fixtures.

There is a regular train service back to Glasgow, so I was in The Horse Shoe Bar by half four to check out the incoming full scores, which was disastrous in regards to my two teams on each side of the River Tyne. My day out was complete with a drink at the Jinglin' Geordie in Edinburgh before catching the 1900 train home.

Another good day north of the border which now takes this project over half way with the total up to 15 from the 27 on the list. I'm satisfied with the progress I'm making and well on course to finish on schedule, but there won't be another trip now until two visits in November and there's already transport obstacles in my path, so it looks like the car will be called into action on my next return.

Matchday Stats

Saturday 19th September (2pm ko)

West of Scotland Central First Division

Johnstone Burgh 2(Heron 73 Hardie 88)

Thorniewood United 0

Att.90hc

Ground no.488

16.Maybe I Should Drive

Hurlford United - Blair Park (November 2015)

There's been a bit of an intermission between my last chapter and this. I know it's just over two months since my last journey to the Joons but it seems much longer. After studying the logistics for all the remaining grounds, I decided that Hurlford would be best done as a road trip. Catching a train to Glasgow, then south to Kilmarnock, or taking the rattler up from Carlisle (that let me down in the Auchinleck chapter) was too much of an inconvenience, especially with a 2-mile bus journey thrown into the mix.

I don't really like driving to football. I much prefer to take public transport, however I don't mind as much if I have some company, so I was pleased to travel up to East Ayrshire with my regular car companions Katie & Lee. Since I introduced you to them at Pollok, I've giving them a nickname and a twitter hashtag of; #NECelebrityGroundhoppingCouple as they have become quite famous around the north-east Non-League scene.

As I was the designated driver, Katie drove up from her home in Houghton-le-Spring for our half nine departure with Lee and her 8-year-old daughter Jade, leaving her car outside my house. Once we crossed the A69 and hit the M6/M74 motorway we stopped off at Gretna Services to check if the match was on. I had Cumnock another club on the list as back up with the safety net of the 3G at Alloa Athletic which would guarantee us a match in Scotland. I rang the Hurlford United club secretary George Jaconelli and he confirmed the match was on after the referee gave the all go after a 10am pitch inspection.

Once we exited the M74 at junction 8, the journey along the A71 took ages through the likes of Stonehouse, Strathaven and Galston, with young Jade constantly asking "Are we there yet" We finally arrived in the one village with two trophies just before 1 o'clock. New road signs were erected by Ayrshire Roads Alliance at the village entrance in recognition of United's 2014 Junior Cup triumph and Hurlford Thistle winning the Scottish Amateur Cup, both within the space of a few weeks. The signs proudly boast HURLFORD One Village - Two Trophies.

Hurlford is in the traditional parish of Riccarton in East Ayrshire, just over 2 miles east of Kilmarnock town centre. The village is found on left bank of the River Irvine and along with the nearby suburb of Crookedholm, has a population of just under 5,000. The area was formerly known as Hurdleford and Whirlford, named because of a ford crossing the river, east of Hurlford Cross near Shawhill. Its Gaelic title Àth Cliath meaning "The Ford of the Hurdles" is also the same Gaelic name as the Irish capital Dublin.

Following the discovery of coal, Hurlford quickly developed in the 19th century. Fireclay and ironstone were also worked extensively at the Eglinton Iron Co, which opened in 1846 until production came to an end in the 1970s. The redeveloped town centre has a ship's propeller erected at the Cross, which serves as a poignant reminder of the town's industrial past.

Hurlford United were first established in 1912, but the current club formed in 1938, winning their first honours in county cup competitions during the 1940s. Before their recent rise to power in the West Region, "The Ford" were historically big in the '70s, when the Bay City Rollers were topping the hit parade and Bowie was about to kill off Ziggy Stardust. In 1972 they won the Ayrshire League Cup again after a 27 year wait, followed by winning the Ayrshire League for the first time in 1972-73, when under the guidance of manager Davie Sneddon, they went the entire league campaign undefeated. During this era, they also added local bragging rights, with more Ayrshire cup honours and achieved a record victory with a 11-0 win over Buckie Rovers in the 2nd round of the Junior Cup in 1974.

The rise through the Junior ranks in recent years is predominantly due to the financial backing of Tarmac man Willie Hamilton which cumulated in The Ford lifting the top prize in 2014. BBC Alba was adding to our TV package which meant for the first time I could watched a Junior Cup game on the tele, as the channel now broadcasting the final live every year.

Hurlford United faced Ayrshire rivals Glenafton Athletic in a match that was over as a contest with just half an hour gone. Stewart Kean gave them a third minute lead for the penalty spot before converting his second from 12 yards in the 29th minute. The former Ayr United and St Mirren striker's first-half strikes came after Ryan McChesney had twice downed Ross Robertson in the box, the second of which resulted in a red card for the defender. So, after being two up against 10 men they coasted to victory with Paul McKenzie nodded home the third for Darren Henderson's United side in the 81st minute to wrap up the victory.

We decided to head straight to the ground for a drink and a bite to eat. After paying our admission we were greeted by George, who had kept a couple of programmes to one side and found us some pin-badges, selling them for two for a fiver instead of the normal three quid, but tipped me the wink and told me not to tell anyone.

Blair Park has a definite village vibe to it. The ground has three steps of terracing on both sides with a small standing cover next to the home dugouts for about 50 spectators. There is a clubhouse selling cans of beer, which I declined as part of my designated driver role, as the laws in Scotland are much stricter regarding drink driving. The ground also has a smashing little snack bar, with the Killie pie being the best matchday pastry based product I consumed in the whole of 2015.

The previous week Hurlford worked like Trojans to get their West of Scotland tie against Renfrew on and they again put the effort in, as the decrepit old groundsman was using what little strength he had to roll the mud-covered goalmouth just before the kick off. Hurlford faced a Falkirk Juniors side, who were sitting 7th in the East Premier, the equivalent of one league below The Ford, who went into this Scottish Junior Cup 3rd Round tie as second favourites to lift the famous trophy at the end of the season.

The hosts applied the pressure from kick-off, the difference in league status was evident as they missed a host of good chances to take an early strong hold on the tie. Following a backs against the wall guard from Falkirk they actually came closest to breaking the deadlock when a quick break from another Ford attack saw an effort from James McAteer come back of the foot of the post.

That near miss was just the kick up the arse the team in the red and white stripes needed, as a brace from Stewart Kean just before the interval set them on their way into round four. On 34 minutes the striker picked up the ball on the edge of the box and played a quick one-two, before firing home from 12 yards, then ten minutes later a low right wing cross from Robertson found Kean at the near post, his initial flicked effort rebounded back off his leg and trickled over the line.

It was 3-0 early in the second half when a ball played in from the left by Ryan Borris found Robertson who stabbed the ball in from close range, and from that point they could have racked up a big score if it wasn't for the Falkirk 'keeper pulling off some terrific saves to keep the score line looking respectable.

With just under ten minutes remaining Falkirk substitute Alan Sneddon was tripped in the box and McAteer calmly fired in the resulting spot-kick, which looked a mere consolation goal, but the away side followed the penalty with a few decent half chances which would have produced a tense finish. In the final minute substitute Ryan Donnelly put the gloss on this cup tie, he picked up the ball on the edge of the box, beat a defender to make himself space to produce a hard-low shot into the bottom right corner of the net which set up a home tie against Dalkeith Thistle in the new year.

The best thing about these 1.45pm kick offs is you can catch up on all the second half action on the radio on the long drive home. Personally, it was a disastrous day with Newcastle losing 3-0 at home to Leicester City, while Gateshead were also gubbed at home, as Halifax Town hammered the Heed 4-1. I fully blame that poor Toon performance at the door of Lee and Katie, because when we've been groundhopping together United lose every time. Lee managed to get the Junior Cup results up on his phone and we were surprised that last year's finalists Musselburgh Athletic had been knocked out. Lee was pleased to see Troon progress as he's developed a soft spot for The Seasiders after they played his favourite Northern League team Seaham Red Star in a pre-season friendly.

Apart from the football results it was a good day out. My aim for the season was a half a dozen clubs off the list each side of Christmas. Hurlford was my fifth of the season plus next week me and the wife are having a weekend break in Glasgow, so I remain on schedule for the 22 grounds over 22 months.

Matchday Stats

Saturday 21st November 2015 (1.45pm ko)

Scottish Junior Cup 3rd Round

Hurlford United 4(Keane 34,44 Robertson 48 Donnelly 90)

Falkirk Juniors 1(McAteer 81)

Att.199hc

Ground no.492

17.Hey Mr Smith

Hill of Beath Hawthorn - Keir's Park (March 2016)

This Scottish Junior project has become a bit disheartening of late, as I've faced postponements on my last two trips to Scotland. After the Hurlford road trip the weekend stay in Glasgow the following week was a total wash out, with my two targets of Arthurlie and Blantyre Victoria both postponed. I still managed to get to a game as the 3G pitch at Petershill Park hosted Rossvale v Dunipace Juniors, this along with Queens Park at Hampden being the only surviving matches in and around Glasgow.

I then went against my decision not to return to Scotland until the spring by driving up to Whitburn Athletic on my January weekend off with Lee and Katie, for what would be my 500th ground. I'll keep what happened on that day on the back burner for now, but I'll just give you a spoiler alert that I was exceedingly pished off!

After these latest setback, I've took a bit time out from the Scottish Joons and debated whether to chuck it or carry on regardless. During that weekend stay in Glasgow we called into The Laurieston pub and got chatting to a lad stood at the bar. When I told him about the book he grabbed me, gave me a big bear hug and actually kissed my hand, as he was so thrilled that someone was writing a book on this subject. He told me he was a Petershill fan, where coincidently I had been to earlier that day. So, after this heart-warming meeting I thought it best to keep going, for his sake just as much as mine.

I'm now more determined to finish this venture before the end of this calendar year, but after the Whitburn setback, I made the sensible decision to hold off heading north until the daffodils have started sprouting from the earth and the thermals are put away in the back of the wardrobe. I booked trains to Edinburgh for my next three Saturday's off in March, April and May, hoping that destiny was on my side with the fixtures. The first of the three worked out great, as Hill of Beath Hawthorn were down for a home fixture on the 19th March.

Hill of Beath is a hill and a village located in between Dunfermline and Cowdenbeath in Fife. The Hill of Beath was the location of a celebrated meeting of the Covenanters, who were a Scottish Presbyterian movement that played an important part in the history of Scotland during the 17th century. At that meeting, held in the summer of 1670 during the height of the struggle against episcopal rule, the Covenanters (including preacher John Blackadder) brought swords and pistols with them to defend themselves against an attack.

The village was built on the hill in the 19th century and owned by the Fife Coal Company, which rented the cottages to the miners during their employment at the colliery. In 1896 the village population was about 1,300, so a public house was built using the Gothenburg system (Eh!..restricted drinking in Scotland) with profits used for public works. The village expanded throughout the last century and the population is now over 11,000.

Hill of Beath is the birthplace of Scottish international Willie Cunningham, who spent 14 years at Deepdale after signing for Preston North End from Airdrie in 1949 and Rangers legend and Scotland captain Jim Baxter. "Slim Jim" was a left sided midfielder who starting his career in 1957 at Raith Rovers before signing for Rangers in 1960, winning ten trophies in his 5 years at Ibrox. Jim signed for the mackems in '65 scoring 12 goals in 98 games, where his heavy drinking reputation would involve a night on the lash before turning out for Sunderland the next day and still playing a blinder! An ex-girlfriend of mine is named after Slim Jim as her Dad was a regular at Roker Park during the sixties. He named his daughter Julie, but giving her a middle name beginning with 'I' to match up with her surname initial of 'M' to spell J.I.M. Coincidently, two days before this trip I bumped into her in the Metrocentre, being the first time we clapped eyes on each other in about 15 years.

Baxter went on to play for Nottingham Forest and finished his career back at Ibrox before retiring in 1970 aged just 31. Jim died of pancreatic cancer in 2001, with his ashes buried at Ibrox Stadium. In 2003, a bronze statue was erected in his honour in Hill of Beath. The £80,000 statue is set in an ornate garden, just outside the football ground and was created by Scottish sculptor Andy Scott.

Hill of Beath Hawthorn F.C. are nicknamed "The Haws" and up until the start of this season, they were managed by Jock Finlayson, who took the job on when the club formed in 1975. The village team have won an array of honours within the Kingdom of Fife over the last forty years, lifting amongst others, the Fife Junior Cup six times and the Fife & Tayside Cup on five occasions. The Haws were Fife

League champions in 1986-87, winning the title a total of nine times, the last of which came in 2004-05.

They currently play in the SJFA East Super League and finished league runners up in 2002-03, 2010-11 and 2011-12. Their Scottish Junior triumph came in 1990 when a goal from Brian Ritchie was enough to defeat Lesmahagow in the final at Rugby Park.

My 0743 from Newcastle arrived in Edinburgh at 0920. I had a pleasant few hours in Edinburgh, visiting my usual cafe, shops and pubs before headed across to Fife on the 1249 Scotrail service to Glenrothes. I got off the train at Cowdenbeath, to be greeted a large police presence at the station and streams of Dunfermline supporters heading to Central Park. I didn't realise the big Fife derby was taking place and the High Street was full of supporters milling around the Goth Bar, which has had a facelift since I last visited Cowdenbeath in April 2011. The 19A bus to Hill of Beath, arriving just a few minutes later so I arrived at Keir's Park just before 2 o'clock. My first call was the Jim Baxter statue, where I took a few photographs for my blog, watched by a couple of blokes having a cigarette outside the Welfare Club.

As I walked towards the club one of the guys said "You've took a photo of a great man"

I quickly replied with "Aye, your right ... even though he played for Sunderland!"

Keir's Park is a very neat and well maintained ground has two terraced standing enclosures on each side. There is shallow terracing behind the goals with turnstile entrances at different parts of the ground. The changing rooms are behind the goal, but no clubhouse so if you want a bevvy there's the neighbouring Welfare Club next to the Jim Baxter statue. At the far turnstile entrance, there's a large plaque on the gate in honour of the club's 1990 Junior Cup success. As I was taking a photo a gentleman approached me and said he would get himself in the picture and introduced himself as Jock, the club manager for 40 years. It was an honour to meet this club legend and told me about calling it a day at the end of the previous season and hoped I would enjoy the game and my visit to the ground.

Hill of Beath Hawthorn who were in tenth spot in the Super League were up against Linlithgow Rose, who weren't having the best of seasons in the East region Superleague by their high standards, sitting in fourth position, however they've enjoyed some cracking adventures in the senior cup this season. They became the first Junior club to reach the last 16 of the Scottish Cup, the highlight of which was a replay win at Forfar Athletic, before losing in the 5th round at Ross County.

It seemed wherever I go nowadays I see someone who I know, so no surprise to find Viking 'Hopper Anders Johansen at the match on another of his football tours from Norway to attend 25 matches in 21 days in all corners of the UK. However more of a coincidence was a Linlithgow fan mentioning my Gateshead FC sweatshirt as I queued for a coffee before the game. The lad told me he was originally from Gateshead and as we spoke to one another it dawned on us both that we knew each other.

"Your Smith… erm..Smiddy isn't it?"

I then recognised him as well, it was Mickey who used to live on the same housing estate as me and we knocked around together in our early teens. Michael moved up the

Scotland 25 year ago, married, and has lived in Linlithgow for the past two decades, so has adopted the Rosey Posey as his team. He also had his young son with him for the game, he mentioned he got him into supporting Linlithgow at a young age to keep him away from the temptation of the Old Firm. His son listened to our conversion, before piped up with "Dad he talks the same way as Grandad does"

Thinking back I first met Mickey in 1978, as he was a neighbour of my mate Sean "Windy" Milligan (he farted a lot). We used to play Subbuteo at Windy's house and play football together on the local school field. Small world, isn't it?

As for the match, the visitors made a good start to the game and deservingly took the lead on 25 minutes, when a free kick from the edge of the box was cleared, before the ball was quickly recycled into the area finding Blair Batchelor unmarked with a diving header. The Rose should have had the game wrapped up by halftime, having two goals adjudged offside by the flag of the linesman and were punished for being lackadaisical in front of goal. Just before the break it was all square, when a cross from the right was headed into his own net by the Linlithgow defender as he attempted to clear from the goal line. This spurred The Haws on in the second half, producing a much better performance and picking up the three points with a peach of a goal. Just after the hour mark Greg Smith picked up the ball on the left flank, cut inside and placed a superb left foot shot from outside the box into the far corner of the net. A goal good enough to grace a cup final, but unfortunately will only be remembered by the 290 or so spectators on a glorious late autumn day in Fife.

After the game, I caught the bus back to Cowdenbeath and as I sat on the platform waiting for the train back to Edinburgh I heard a roar from the direction of Central Park, which turned out to be the only goal of the game as The Pars beat the Blue Brazil in the local derby.

A day and a chapter full of coincidences concluding just before I headed home for the 1830 train. I found out my best mate Zippy and his girlfriend Helen were staying in Edinburgh for the weekend, so I met up with them for a pint in the Jingling Geordie. As I was alluded to earlier. It's a very very small world, isn't it?

Matchday Stats

Saturday 19th March 2016 (2.30pm ko)

East Region Super League

Hill of Beath Hawthorn 2 (OG 40 Smith 61)

Linlithgow Rose 1 (Batchelor 25')

Att.290hc

Ground no.512

18. Road, River and Rail

Tayport - The Canniepairt (April 2016)

The fixtures were falling into place perfectly, as my next train excursion to Edinburgh gave me a few different options. The standout fixture was at Tayport, not because of the particular game but it gave me a chance to knock off one of the far-flung destinations.

James contacted me a few days beforehand to let me know that he would pick up at noon at our usual rendezvous point at the Market Street entrance to Waverley Station. He also informed me that there had been heavy rainfall all week so suggested some backup games with 3G pitches on route to Tayport, just in case it was postponed. This wasn't an option for me, it was shit or bust as far as I was concerned, Tayport would have to be on and I told him it better be or he would see a grown man cry.

Tayport is a small harbour town and burgh close to the north-east tip of Fife, originally known by its Gaelic name Partan Craig, which translates as "Crab Rock". By 1415 it was known as Portincragge and as Port-in-Craige by the end of the 15th century, then in 1598 the settlement received its burgh charter in the name of Ferry-Port on Craig.

The Edinburgh, Perth and Dundee Railway Company established a railway service running from Edinburgh to Aberdeen in the 1850s that stopped in the town. They used the much simpler name of "Tayport" which soon caught on and eventually replaced Ferry-Port on Craig as the more commonly used name. The motto of the Burgh is "Te oportet alte ferri" which translates as "It is incumbent on you to carry yourself high" ...What the fu...???

Tayport looks north across the River Tay to Broughty Ferry and the 15th century Broughty Castle. To the east is the vast Tentsmuir Nature Reserve, an area of forested dunes and moorland which covers 50 square miles. The town is renowned for the line fishing industry, one of the oldest in Scotland, which once-upon-a-time time gave employment to approximately 45,000 men. The ferry service across the Tay was already well established by the 12th century when these lands were granted to the newly formed Arbroath Abbey. The abbey constructed shelter and lodgings for pilgrims travelling between St Andrews and Arbroath via the ferry and this formed the centre of a settlement that steadily grew over the centuries.

The population increased at the end of the 18th century with houses built to take advantage of jobs in the town's textile and shipbuilding industries. The ferry service was obtained by the railway in 1851, which used the route for a railway ferry service from Edinburgh to Aberdeen. The service ceased once the Tay Rail Bridge opened in 1878, but quickly resumed the following year when the bridge collapsed. The replacement bridge meant Tayport returned to a passenger-only ferry in 1887, which continued to run from the town to Broughty Ferry until 1920. The opening of the new Tay Road Bridge in 1966 put Tayport within a few minutes' drive of the centre of Dundee, and since then it's evolved into a pleasant commuter town for that city over the River Tay, with a population of just under 8,000.

Football in Tayport stretches back prior to the First World War, with a Junior club in the town winning the East of

Fife Cup in 1905. There's been several different amateur teams in the subsequent years, with the principal club after the Second World War being Tayport Violet. In 1947 a new club, Tayport Amateurs was formed as rivals to Violet by a bunch of local lads who had been playing friendlies together as a boy's scouts team. This was the birth of the club we know today, beginning life in the Midlands Amateurs' Alliance League, where they soon climbed the leagues before becoming toe-to-toe rivals with Tayport Violet. Both clubs won promotion to the top division, but after the 1952-53, season which saw Violet finish runners-up to YM Anchorage (who had won the title 20 years on the bounce) they called it a day, leaving the Amateurs as the town's only club.

Throughout the fifties and sixties, the club's fortunes were mixed but they managed to survive some desperate times, until a new club committee formed in the late sixties, which steered the club in the right direction, enjoying relative success through the next two decades.

In 1990 the club's Junior team was launched and at the same time a name change, becoming simply 'Tayport Football Club', a handle which covered both the amateur and junior grades. By the turn of the millennium enthusiasm for amateur football in the town diminished, so season 2000–2001 was to be the club's last in the Amateurs Leagues. The club could now focus all their attention on the all-conquering Junior side, who enjoyed phenomenal success from the 1990s, winning the Tayside Premier League nine times in eleven seasons. Their switch to the East Region Superleague couldn't halt the trophy haul, winning the division in 2002-03 and 2005-06, with two runners-up spots in between.

The Port's love affair with the Junior Cup came during this era, appearing in half of the finals during a twelve-year period between 1993 and 2005. After losing by the only goal of the game against Glenafton in 1993, they lifted the trophy for the first time three years later when a brace from Stephen Ross paved the way to a 2-0 success over Camelon. They were back the following year, but again they had to settle for runners-up medals after losing the final 2-1 to Pollok. Between 2003 and 2005 they played in three consecutive finals, winning the trophy, with a goal by Craik enough to overcome Linlithgow Rose and beating Lochee United 2-0, with Henderson and Middleton on target to take the trophy back to Fife. They were denied what would have been a trophy hat-trick by a penalty shoot-out defeat to Carnoustie after the 2004 final finished goalless.

My panic of another pending postponement waned when I arrived in Edinburgh just after 11 o'clock to be was greeting by bright sunshine, however this didn't stop me being a paranoid nutter, fearful of another wasted trip by checking twitter every 15 minutes to see if the match was on.

The date for this trip coincided with what used the be one of my favourite days of the year, as the third Saturday in April to us audiophiles is known as 'Record Store Day' This annual event started in 2007, to celebrate the culture and promote independently owned record shops. The day brings together fans, artists, and thousands of independent worldwide record stores with the release of several records especially pressed for distributed to shops participating in the event. Nowadays I don't bother with it, if there's any record released that I want I just go over to Newcastle on the following Monday, where I can usually pick up what I need. However, with exclusive releases from the likes of

Justin Bieber and One Direction, the whole RSD ethos has somewhat lost its cool, having lost its original purpose and becoming more of a record label cash cow.

The 60 mile drive across to Fife, via the A90 and A91, included a refreshment break in the charming Fife town of Cupar, calling for a drink in The Boudingait, where I enjoyed a pint of Orkney 'Corncake Ale'. The whole journey was perfectly timed, arriving at the ground with half an hour to spare before the 2.30 kick off.

The local council invited The Port to move from East Common to this former farm land in 1975. The ground has a covered terrace enclosure running down on one side, behind the home dugout, the away club dugout is on the opposite side in front of a grass banking standing area. The changing rooms are behind the goal where there's open hardstanding. At the top goal, there is a large hedge which makes it a three-sided ground.

Tayport were relegated from the Super League in 2013-14, but made a quick return winning the East Region Premier League at the first attempt. Their stay in the top league is a brief one as they looked like a team hurling towards the drop after a heavy home defeat to Linlithgow Rose.

When I saw Linlithgow away at Hill of Beath recently they created a hatful of chances in the early stages but failed to capitalise on their dominance. This looked to again be the case as they carved through the Port defence without finding the onion bag, that was until the 24th minute, when the ball was slipped into the box to Tommy Coyne, who produced a nice finish into the roof of the net.

As the match approached the half an hour mark I realised the home team were still to reach the opposition's penalty area, then suddenly a cross field pass found Alan Tulleth unmarked on the left wing in acres of space, who had time to pick his spot and fire in a hard-low shot into the far corner. The faint hope that the hosts could get a result from the fixture lasted less than a minute, when a right-wing ball found Colin Strickland in the box, who had time and space to slot home. Then five minutes before the interval he latched onto a long ball down the middle of the park, which the keeper didn't come to meet which made an easy finish for the Rosey number nine.

At half time, we had a chat to a couple of lady Linlithgow supports who quizzed us on our groundhopping and we also discussed Junior football in general. They seemed really pleased that someone was writing a book on the subject, as they said that no one has really bothered in the past. We also popped into the clubhouse, as I was keen to see the club memorabilia and pick up the odd fact or two for the book. The club official initially blocked our entry, as it's for season tickets only, but he reluctantly gave in to our request of a quick look inside. He seemed in a foul mood, but I'm guessing it was due to his team's first half performance and pending relegation to the East Premier League than any vendetta against a couple of them daft Groundhopping types.

For the second half, we watched the game at the other side of the ground, in the covered terrace which turned out to be a cracking decision, as it lashed down during the second half. A half which saw Tommy Coyne head in a right-wing cross from six yards on the hour and late into the game substitute Conor Kelly capitalise on a comedy of errors in the Port box to make it 5-1.

On the return journey back to Edinburgh, we listened to the football updates on Five Live. I was obviously delighted with Newcastle's 3-0 win over Swansea City. but didn't get too excited about the result, as I know just like the club I visited today, that our relegation fate is already sealed. However, I'm confident that The Toon's stay in the second tier of English football is a brief one and I'm guessing that Tayport feel the same, that it's just a holiday from the top division and a return to the East Region Super League is imminent.

Matchday Stats

Saturday 16th April 2016 (2.30pm ko)

East Region Super League

Tayport 1(Tulleth 30)

Linlithgow Rose 5(Coyne 24,60 Strickland 31,40 Kelly 87)

Att.175

Ground no.515

19. Live in A Hiding Place

Glenafton Athletic - Loch Park (April 2016)

My pre-season target to knock off at least ten chapters for this book has falling way short, with only seven ticked as we approach the end of April. To make matters worse I've only one work free Saturday left before the end of the season, with return trains to Edinburgh already trousered for the middle of May.

I booked leave for the last week in April, as I was going to a Groundhop in Nottingham for the weekend, attending five matches in the Notts Senior League, with one game on Friday night and four spread across the Saturday. This event was organised by Rob Hornby, the Mansfield based 'hopper is legendary in organising these football bonanzas and this was to be his last, deciding to retire because of health reason and to devote more time to his family.

As I was missing out on another trip from the Toon to the Scottish Joons, I checked out the midweek fixtures when they were finally revealed, and noted that Glenafton Athletic were at home to Auchinleck Talbot on the Monday night. This was a good trip to do by car, with an early evening kick-off and about a 3-hour drive, which is quicker and a hell of a lot cheaper by road than rail. Lee and Katie were available to accompany me, so they headed up to my abode for a 2pm departure.

My planned route was the A69 to Carlisle, then come off the M74 and head across the A75 to Dumfries for something to eat. The trip was going well until the traffic came to an abrupt halt on the motorway. After five minutes, we realised there must have been an accident much further ahead, but luckily, I managed to turn off on a nearby junction, so Lee could navigate me back onto the A75 further on and clear of the incident, otherwise our stomachs would have remained empty and we might have been pushing it to make the match on time.

The obvious stopping point for bait was The Robert the Bruce, the Weatherspoon's pub is one I thought I had been to before when I saw Newcastle play a friendly against Queen of the South in 2003, however when I got there I realised I had never set foot in the place, so had mistakenly ticked it off. While in the pub I got a message from Mark Wilkins, my favourite cockney saying he was also going to the game, so this kept up my recent record of seeing someone I know wherever I go, in whatever part of the UK that may be.

Glenafton Athletic play in the parish and former mining town of New Cumnock in East Ayrshire. The town's growth came during the 20th century with several pits and miner's rows expanding this small town into a mining community, which now has a population of just under 3,000.

The Knockshinnoch Castle Colliery was sunk in 1942 on the site of a former pit which had been dispensed with 60 years earlier. In September 1950, thirteen people were killed and 129 miners were trapped by a landslide. Two years later a film was produced about the disaster called The Brave Don't Cry, starring John Gregson, John Rae, Meg Buchanan and directed by Philip Leacock. The film was shot at Southall Studios, using actors from the Glasgow Citizen's Theatre and there now lies a memorial at the former site of the colliery.

New Cumnock has an interesting history, with links to the three principal men in Scottish history: William Wallace, Robert the Bruce and Robbie Burns.

Scottish Makar Blind Harry's 'romantic poem' - The Wallace or to give it the full title - The Actes and Deidis of the Illustre and Vallyeant Campioun Schir William Wallace, placed the Mel Gibson lookalike in and around the village four times in his valiant tales of the patriot. The poem was written in the late 15th century and refers to Wallace in the area between 1296 up until his betrayal in July 1305. The text refers to the village as Cumno and his household at 'Blak Crag', in the lands of Blackcraig in the upper reaches of the Afton Water

Robert the Bruce has much stronger links to area, after he was crowned King of the Scots in 1306, he suffered early setbacks against the English military, forcing him to seek refuge in the Western Isles and in Ireland. Bruce and his followers returned to the mainland the following year, overcoming English forces at Glen Trool and later Loudon Hill under the command of Sir Aymer de Vallence, before again taking refuge, choosing New Cumnock because of the 'strenthis' - i.e. the steepness of the Blackcraig and Craigbraneoch hills in Glen Afton.

Here he was joined by Sir James Douglas, who warned Bruce of the pending attack from the English garrison assembled at Cumnock Castle, led by de Vallence along with John of Lorn, the sworn enemy of Bruce. Lorn had brought with him a sleuth-hound which had once belonged to the King of the Scots, to help track down his former master. This tactic came to no avail, for Bruce and his 'four hundred men' evaded capture 'up in the strenthis' - the hills of New Cumnock.

Edward I of England and his heir Edward II both tried in vain to find and capture Bruce as he continued to lay low in the south-west hills. Evading arrest he and his men could break free and overcome his enemies within Scotland. Edward II returned at the head of another army only to be outdone by Bruce again, defeated at the Battle of Bannockburn, in June 1314.

Scotland's national bard Robert Burns was a frequent visitor, especially in his youth and he immortalise the Afton Water which flows into the River Nith with his 1791 poem 'Sweet Afton'

Flow gently, sweet Afton! amang thy green braes,

Flow gently, I'll sing thee a song in thy praise;

My Mary's asleep by thy murmuring stream,

Flow gently, sweet Afton, disturb not her dream.

Football first came to the fore within the coal-mining community in 1877, with the formation of colliery team Lanemark F.C. who played at Connel Park in the heart of miners' rows. In those early football days, matches were either cup competitions or friendly fixtures, as league football struggled. Throughout those formative years' other clubs came and went within the parish, before the first Junior club was formed in the 1920's in the shape of New Cumnock United, who played on the Connel Park pitch, which was now owned by New Cumnock Collieries Ltd. The club were successful, winning the South Ayrshire League three times before the downfall in coal demand and the pending General Strike, saw the club fold before the decade was out.

Glenafton Athletic formed in 1930 and take their name from the Glen Afton, through which sweetly flows the Afton water. The coal industry was thriving again and the new club made an instant impact in the Junior game, winning the South Ayrshire League, before switching to the Western League which they won at the first attempt and adding a host of cup honours to boot. Following the war the club went through a lean spell until winning the title again in 1959, then after 30 years playing at Connel Park, they moved to a new ground at Loch Park in 1960, and at the same time changed the club colours from black and white to red. The dawn of a new era saw a hat-trick of league titles and their first appearance in the Junior Cup final, the Glens losing 2-1 to Irving Meadow in the 1963 final at Hampden Park.

The club came to prominence again during the 1990's under the leadership of Alan Dunlop in partnership with Alan Rough, Scotland's most capped goalkeeper and one of the bubble perm squad from Argentina '78. During this era, they played in 3 consecutive Scottish Junior Cup finals between 1992 and 1994, their only success being a goal from John Miller against Tayport in the '93 final, in a season winning treble of the Ayrshire League and Cup. Each side of that success they lost out to fellow Ayrshire clubs Auchinleck Talbot and Largs Thistle, with their most recent appearance in 2014, losing 3-0 to Hurlford United in another all Ayrshire final.

Overall, they have won the rebooted Ayrshire League three times and in 2011- season they were winners of West of Scotland Super League First Division, to go with a bucket full of winner's medals in Ayrshire cup competitions.

The road from Dumfries is via the A76 zigzag road which took us just under an hour. We arrived at the car park opposite the ground entrance at the same time as Mark Wilkins who was staying in Carlisle, using the border town as a base to see a few more games this week. On entering the ground, you find a 250-capacity covered stand on one side, filled with bench seats and named in honour of Mick Morran, the club's late physio. At each side of the stand there is plenty of terracing, with the rest of the ground open with sleeper terracing and grass banking, including the strange site of the TV gantry being used as some kind of dog pen. This was one of the weirdest sights I've ever seen on my travels. I took a few pictures and the dogs didn't seem too keen on having their photo taking, barking at me in a manner which suggested they wanted me to Eff off! (They must have known I was a Postman)

There's a clubhouse bar in the Hugh Campbell Hall, named after the former club president. The changing rooms are behind the goal in the Hunter Pavilion, which has a trophy room and hospitality upstairs. One of the club officials saw me taking some pre-match pictures and realising I was a traveller, so he showed me the fresh plans for a new changing facility and an all-weather playing surface.

Glenafton Athletic went into the match with Auchinleck Talbot in fourth spot, with their opponents looking poised to clinch their fourth consecutive West Super League Premier Division title. Backed by a healthy following from 8 miles up the road, the Bot ran out comfortable winners with a goal in each half. Graham Wilson got on the end of a left-wing cross at the far post, sliding the ball past the 'keeper from close range on 29 minutes, then early in the second period when a precise direct free-kick from 20 yards, left of the penalty area was fired into the top right hand corner by Dwayne Hyslop. This victory saw Talbot leapfrog Troon at to the top of the division, and with still four games in hand over their nearest rivals, they were well on course to win a fifth Super League Premier title.

Although it was quite a nippy evening (why on earth did I think it would be warm because it's April) it was an enjoyable one. Everyone at the club and the few supporters I spoke to were very cordial, the only hostility coming from the dogs lurking menacingly in the scaffold tower. It was good to meet up with Mark at the game and good of Lee and Katie to come along, although they wouldn't refuse the chance of another ground to tick off. The return journey home went without a hitch, so I was back at HQ at 11.20pm, satisfied with another club scratched off the list.

Matchday Stats

Monday 25h April 2016 (6.45pm ko)

West Region - Super League Premier Division

Glenafton Athletic 0

Auchinleck Talbot 2(Wilson 29 Hyslop 56)

Att.250.est

Ground no.517

20. The Hard One

Carnoustie Panmure - Laing Park (May 2016)

The task of visiting all the winning clubs over the last 50 years, was made so much easier with the trophy switching between the East and West Regions. In fact, within this period, there hasn't even been a defeated finalist from the North Region. The last club to make the final from the top half of the country were Aberdeen based Banks O' Dee, who defeated Kilsyth Rangers 1-0 in the 1957 final.

This means that the most northerly club to win it since then are Carnoustie Panmure. In 2001 they faced Renfrew, followed by Tayport three years later with both finals finishing goalless after extra time and decided by the dreaded penalties. If you're paying attention to what you've already read in the previous chapters, you will already know that they lost the first final 6-5 on spot-kicks, but lifted the trophy in 2004 winning 4-1 in the shootout.

Carnoustie is a small town in between Dundee and Arbroath, which sits at the mouth of the Barry Burn on the Angus coast with a population of over 11,000. There are a few variations on the origin of its name, suggestions include various Gaelic derivations, translated to 'fort, rock or cairn of the feast,' or 'cairn of the firtree' and it's also been suggested Carnoustie may derive from 'Càrn Ùstaidh' an obscure Pictish element. There's also the Anglic origin 'Craws Nestie', referring to the large number of crows that inhabit the area, however the best, but more unlikely possibility is 'the Cairn of Heroes', which refers to a battle fought there in 1010 between Malcolm II and the Danish

Vikings. The Battle of Barry took place at Lochty Burn near the area which is now occupied by the High Street. The Viking onslaught was led by Camus, who fled to the hills, but was slain and buried by Robert de Keith at Brae Downie. Carnoustie has a street named after him and the Camus Cross is said to record his resting place.

The town was founded in the late 18th century, growing rapidly throughout the 19th century due to the development of the local linen industry, especially the opening of The Panmure Works by James Smieton in 1857, where he also provided new housing on several streets and opened the Panmure Works Institute on Kinloch Street.

Due to its seaside location, it became a popular tourist resort from the early Victorian era, benefited from the 19th century fashion for sea bathing, then following the arrival of the railway it was promoted as the "Brighton of the North" a tagline which they definitely wouldn't go with in the 21st century for one obvious reason.

Any mention of the small town of Carnoustie will instinctively make you think of golf and the famous Carnoustie Golf Links course which first hosted The Open Championship in 1931, and will again play host for the eighth time in 2018. The course has historically proved a magnetic challenge for golfers of all standards, giving the nickname of "Car-nasty" by the Americans, due to its difficulty and the added hurdle of the adverse Scottish weather. It was the scene of Paul Lawrie's heroics in the 1999 Open, when the lad from Aberdeen lifted the famous claret jug in front of his home crowd.

The town is the birthplace of actor Ian McDiarmid, best known for his recurring role as Emperor Palpatine aka

Darth Sidious in the Star Wars films, depicted as an aged, ash faced, cloaked wearing villain (A bit like myself after a heavy session on the lash) Also Dundee born photographer Iain Macmillan, whose most famous snap is the iconic cover of The Beatles' Abbey Road album (which along with the White Album is my favourite long player from the fab four) He returned north to live in Carnoustie in 1980, where he lived until his death from lung cancer in 2006.

Formed in 1936, Carnoustie Panmure Football Club are nicknamed "The Gowfers" due to the town's well-established links to golf. They replaced the long standing Carnoustie Juveniles club, so a new team could play in the preferred Dundee Leagues, instead of the Angus League. The club originally played on a park beside the old slaughterhouse until 1947, when they moved to Westfield Road and at the same time changed the club colours from green and gold to red and white.

The old ground was donated by the late Mr. Edgar Thomson of D.C.Thomson's, with the pitch constructed completely by the Club Committee. The football pitch was put together with turf carted from the Links by the late Mr Fairlie Hovell, who ran a motor lorry at that time and was a big fan of the Gowfers, both home and away, even when he was well into his eighties. Former Carnoustie stalwart Jock Thompson brought his Manchester City side to Tayside for its official opening, and he later retired to Carnoustie, becoming licensee of the 19th Hole pub in Kinloch Street.

The Gowfers first run of success came during the fifties, when they were christened "The Arsenal of the North" because of their similar red with white sleeve shirts. The club were Dundee Junior League champions on five occasions during the decade, and they also won the title twice during the mid-sixties. More silverware followed during the 1970s, lifting the Tayside Premier Division title four years on the bounce from 1975-76 season and topping the table for a fifth time in 1981, as well as adding plenty of pots and cups within the Tayside area.

The club re-emerged as a force in the East Region at the turn of the new century after receiving significant investment in the late 1990s. The pinnacle came with those two Junior Cup final appearances at the beginning of this century.

In 2012 the club joined forces with Carnoustie YM AFC, Carnoustie Panmure Youth FC and Monifieth Ladies FC, to form Carnoustie Panmure FC as a Scottish Charitable Incorporated Organisation. This provides a pathway for players from youth to adult football and to also improve sports facilities within the town. In 2013 the joint club became the first to receive the Scottish FA Legacy Club Award in the SFA East Region and they now have 350 players on the roster across 18 teams in various age groups.

My hardest and longest trip was just over 200 miles, which isn't as far as it looks on the map. The distance split between taking the train from the Toon to the capital, followed by a lift from my ever-reliable Edinburgh chauffeur James Little. After boarding the 0743 from Newcastle, I had a few hours spare to visit my usual haunts around the city before James picked me up on Market Street at 11.30. As is usually the case, he'd chosen a refreshment pit stop along the route, so the 73-mile drive to Angus was divided up by a drink in the Glencarse Hotel just off the A90 motorway. We made good time along the

A92, allowing us a visit to the Corner Hotel in Carnoustie before kick-off. The pub was full of red and white scarves, which I thought was a home supporters bar, but they were all in fact Bonnyrigg fans. One of which was an old acquaintance of James, a lad called John Young who he used to regularly play 5-a-side with, who was at the game to watch his son Kerr, who plays centre-half for Rose.

This is the club's third ground, having started life playing on a park pitch next to the slaughterhouse until moving to Westfield Road in 1947. In 2004 they relocated to a brand-new facility at Laing Park, which at the car park entrance is signed as Pitskelly Park, which is the name only used by the local council. The changing rooms, refreshment bar, club office and dugouts are all down one side at the pay entrance, with the rest of the ground made up of grass banking.

On arrival, I looked up Mark Johnson the club General Manager, who asked me to come and say hello after seeing my post on Twitter. Mark used to work for neighbouring Junior club St Andrews, before being asked to get involved with The Gowfers. He hails from Derby, so is naturally a fan of the Rams. His home team were in action earlier in the day, playing Hull City at home in the Championship play-offs, a game that James and I watched in the pub earlier at Glencarse. We saw Hull take an early lead on their way to a 3-0 first leg win, so a bad start to the football day for Mark and it was about the get much worse.

Carnoustie were up against Bonnyrigg Rose, who had one hand on the Superleague title, knowing that a victory coupled with nearest challengers Kelly Hearts dropping points would make them champions. Laing Park was the setting the last time they clinched the East Region Superleague in 2012, so the omens were good for us to witness The Rose claim the title in Angus. The silverware was well on its way back to Midlothian as the visitors, backed by a noisy following, had the three points trousered well before half time. With just seven minutes gone a poor clearance from the 'keeper fell straight to Wayne McIntosh who capitalised by firing in from the edge of the box. Then ten minutes later a deep left wing cross from the left by Donaldson was met by a peach of a header by Kieran McGachie which rattled in the stanchion of the goal. Just before half time they grabbed a third when Lewis Turner was on hand to net the rebound, after the goalkeeper denied McIntosh with a good save. The second half was just a matter of how many, but surprisingly this goal thirsty observer saw just two more, with a superb volley from just outside the box by Jonathan Stewart on 73 minutes and an injury time bullet header by Dean Hoskins to make it 5-0.

The champagne had to be put on ice as Kelty Hearts won 3-1 at Camelon, which meant the Rose needed to lose both remaining matches and Kelty had to win their remaining four fixtures, plus overturn a 20-goal deficit. Two days later the Superleague title was confirmed with a 3-0 win also against Camelon and for good measure they hit four against Penicuik Athletic in their final game. At the bottom end of the table Panmure retained their league status winning two of their remaining five matches to finish in 12th position.

I left Carnoustie without even catching the sight of a wayward "fore" ball. The return journey went smoothly so was back in Edinburgh with an hour to spare for before the 1900 train home, delighted to have now ticked off the furthest grounds in my Scottish Juniors quest. As the season draws to its concluding I'm now beginning to see some light at the end of the tunnel. I've finished the campaign having visited nine of the 27, leaving just seven left to tick off before Christmas, so now feel well on course to finish below par.

Matchday Stats

<u>Saturday 14th May 2016 (2.30pm ko)</u>

East Region Superleague

Carnoustie Panmure 0

Bonnyrigg Rose 5(McIntosh 7 McGauchie 14 Turner 39 Stewart 73 Hoskins 90+3)

Att.250 est

Ground no.526

21. Glittering Prize

Beith Juniors - Bellsdale Park (6th June 2016)

After a lot of begging and pleading on Facebook, I finally got myself fixed up with a lift to this year's Junior Cup Final. The 2016 showdown saw Pollok, who've made great progress on the field since I visited Newlandsfield at the end of last season, up against Beith Juniors, making their first appearance in the Junior showpiece.

An all West Region final meant another trip to Kilmarnock, which is an awkward destination to reach by rail from down our neck of the woods, so it's either travelling to Glasgow first, or taking the slow rattler from Carlisle. This means the car is the only real option, so the offer of a lift was much appreciated, well it wasn't exactly an offer, more of a self-enforced invitation from Harry Watson. I've known Harry for about 10 years, he's a regular down Gateshead Stadium, but is more of a groundhopper with an interest in the Northern League clubs. He is no stranger to Junior football, this being the 20th final he's attended, the first of which was the 1992 final between Auchinleck and Glenafton. He originally hails from Forres in Morayshire, but has happily resided on Tyneside for the last 37 years.

Riding shotgun with us was Ivan Hay who I first met in 2009 when Gateshead played away at Forest Green Rovers on the opening day of the season. After a family holiday in Tenerife, I jetted back into Newcastle in the early hours and after a few hours' kip, jumped into a 16-seater minibus for a 600-mile round trip to Gloucestershire. I sat next to

Ivan on the bus and found him great company, discovering he had completed 'The 92' and the set of Scottish senior grounds. I often see Ivan at matches around the north-east, enjoying a chat and a catch up on where he's been and what he's been up to.

We had a great day at the final, arriving in the ground early for a Killie Pie (while they're still hot and fresh) and an Empire biscuit, before meeting up with Jamie McQueen and John Blair who had travelled over from Edinburgh. Also at the game was Groundhopping legend, Lawrence Reade and his girlfriend Robyn. Their journey north was a hell of a lot longer than ours, as Lawro comes from Oxford, while Robyn lives in Bristol, but they made a full weekend of it by ticking off Bo'ness United the day before. We managed to get seats together in the West Stand, amongst the Pollok supporters, as it's at this point that I have to make the confession I wanted the 'Lok to win the trophy for the fourth time. The simple reason for this was a Beith victory would mean another ground to visit, so a case of two steps forward, one step back in trying to finish this quest of winners of this famous old trophy.

It looked like I may have got my wish as Pollok set the pace during the first half, creating a handful of decent chances but were unable to break the deadlock. After the restart, it appeared that the Beith players must have either received a half time rollicking or some boost of inner confidence, as they looked so much sharper and the team most likely to nick the lead. Their good spell of pressure was rewarded on 61 minutes when a long ball from the defence found Darren Christie, who shook off his marker Chris Walker, before firing a low hard left foot drive across the goalkeeper and into the far corner of the net. He raced to celebrate with the Cabes supporters housed in the East

Stand. I read an interview online after the match and he said "It was just good to score in front of all my mates in that far corner," "There was a full bus of them there and my mum with my wee girl as well so it was great to score on that side."

The goal stunned Pollok, giving them a kick up the backside and a sudden rush of urgency, so just over ten minutes it was all square, when 41-year-old Pollok legend Robbie Winters scored just 30 seconds after coming off the bench. He fired in the rebound after the initial shot from his younger brother came back off the post, which set up a grand finale. The large Rugby Park pitch took its toll on both teams, with the best chance falling to Thomas Collins who headed wide in injury time, so the match fizzled out with the teams deadlocked after ninety minutes.

When the referee blew for full time I knew there was only going to be one winner. For the first time in the Junior Final there wasn't the usual half an hour of extra time, instead the final would immediately be settled by who has the most bottle and can hold their nerve to fire in a free shot from 12 yards, and I sensed that this team was Beith. My penalty shootout wisdom seemed incorrect, when Pollok converted both their efforts, sandwiched in between a soft arsed effort straight at Longmuir from Kenny McLean. Collins made it 2-1 to keep the Mighty in with a shout, before the whole scenario switch around with Grindlay saving the next two kicks from Allan McKenzie and David Winter. It was finally left up to Richie Burke to take the last of the allotted ten spot kicks and he made no mistake to make it 4-3 to Beith. Claiming a victory in the year of the underdog, which has saw Leicester City overcoming the mega rich big guns to win the title in England for the first time, Hibs winning the Scottish Cup after a 104 year wait and now a new name on the Junior Cup.

During the drive home I sat cramped up in the back of Harry's Fiat Panda debating if it would be possible to tick Beith in the last few weeks of the season, as I didn't want another ground to be added to the list for next season. I knew they were at home on the following Saturday against Auchinleck Talbot in the Ayrshire Weekly Press Cup quarter-final, but that four-letter word - work, meant it wasn't possible, so I would have to wait and see.

My travel companions Lee and Katie along with Facebook legend John McClure travelled up to Beith six days later for that cup tie. They posted pictures on my 100 Grounds Club Facebook page, and I was green with envy when I saw them posing with the holy grail of Scottish Junior football in the club boardroom. They had home fixtures lined up the following week on both Monday and Wednesday, so I tweeted the official Beith Juniors twitter feed to ask if the trophy would be on display again this week, when they confirmed it would be I decided to drive up by myself on Monday afternoon for their final league fixture of the season against, as fate would have it - Pollok.

I didn't fancy the long 172-mile drive to North Ayrshire, but a glorious hot summer day made the decision an easy one, so after work I went to bed for an hour before setting off at 3.30pm. The trip ran smoothly, even negotiating the rush hour traffic along the M8 to reach the A737 without any problems, so I safely arrive at Bellsdale Park in exactly 3 hours from my front door to theirs.

The small town of Beith has a population of just under 7,000, situated in the east side of the Garnock Valley in

North Ayrshire, approximately 20 miles south-west of Glasgow. The town name originates from Old Irish for birch tree, as the district was originally covered with woods and known as 'Hill of Beith'

The town has historical links to smuggling especially during the 18th century, gaining a reputation for harbouring bad 'uns, due to its location between the coast and Paisley and Glasgow. In 1733 around fifty Beith smugglers ravaged the Irvine Customs House, escaping with a rich booty of confiscated contraband goods and by 1789 a company of 76 soldiers were quartered to police the town to try and combat the continuing illegal trade in tobacco, tea and spirits. The Smugglers Tavern on Main Street pays homage to the days when Beith was an expedient stopping point for villains. Also, a possible passage for moving these goods through Beith is the ley tunnel that is said to run from Eglinton Street to Kilbirnie Loch.

Beith Juniors formed in 1938 and play in the classic and best kit there is - black and white striped shirts and are nicknamed The Cabes or The Mighty. They were champions of the West of Scotland Premier Division in 2009–10, and previously the Ayrshire League twice during the sixties and North Ayrshire League Section winners five times during the same decade. The club lifted the West of Scotland Cup in 1966 and '67 and finally again in 2009, with the Ayrshire Cup claimed on nine occasion plus plenty of other district and county cup honours.

There was an original Beith FC, who formed in 1875 and played at senior level. The club moved from Kersland Field, Glengarnock to Bellsdale Park in 1920, with the Junior club taking over the ground after they succeeded the disbanded club to join the Western League North Division for the 1939–40 season. The ground has two standing enclosures on the far side, decked out in black and white which the novelty of 3G grass on the terraces. There is another standing enclosure on the main side, with the dressing rooms in the bottom corner and the turnstile entrance at the top of the hefty slope. The boardroom bar and snack bar are next to the entrance with open areas behind both goals, with a scattering of bench seats throughout.

On arrival, my priority was to seek out the trophy and get the much-needed photo I desired with the old silver pot. I asked in the boardroom bar where it was and was told it wasn't on show for tonight's game as they were playing Pollok, so they didn't want to appear to be rubbing their noses in it. As you can imagine my heart sank with this news, it was like a kick in the bollocks, but I fully understood their decision and admired the respect shown to their opponents. When I told the lad behind the bar what I was doing and how far I'd travelled he quickly had a word with club secretary Robert McCarter, who took me to see a guy called John, who as luck would have it, had the trophy in the boot of his car. He passed his keys onto his pal Jim, who took me out to the car park, taking the trophy and plinth out of their boxes and taking some photos with me posing proudly with the Scottish Holy Grail in my mitts.

I was really chuffed with this, so special thanks to everyone involved, I know to them it might have seemed a cheeky request, but it was very much appreciated and yet another reason why these clubs have been a joy to visit and this book a pleasure to write.

After getting stuck into a fabulous chicken & haggis pie (without a doubt the best pie I've had so far this year and a number one contender for my 'scabby-eye of the year' award for 2016) I settled down for the match, sitting on the bench seat behind the goal with some folk from Port Glasgow, who were Morton fans and were terrific company during the game.

Prior to kick off Pollok showed their class by providing a guard of honour to the triumphant Junior Cup winners as they entered the pitch. The match itself was a typical end of season affair, with both teams prioritising forthcoming cup semi-finals, with much changed line-ups from the big game just over a week ago.

This turned out to be my 114th and final fixture of the 2015-16 season, the clubs involved came up with the same result as my penultimate match with one goal apiece. The home side took the lead on 35 minutes after good work by the young Beith 'keeper Scott Walker, who set McGowan on his way down the left wing. He provided an inch perfect cross for Thomas Collins to fire in from six yards. Pollok equalised early in the second half when a left-wing cross was met by a cheeky back heel from Del Hepburn from close range. Shouts of "Mon the Mighty" from the home contingent couldn't provide a winner, so the final match of the season resulted in Beith finishing in 7th spot with Pollok just ahead of them in 5th.

The season finished on a high for both clubs after safely coming through their semi-finals 48 hours later. Beith completed a cup double by winning a tenth Ayrshire Cup with a 5-1 victory over Irving Meadow, while Pollok lifted the Central League Cup gubbing Greenock 7-1.

On the final whistle, I was quickly out of the ground and on the road for the long trek home, content with a great night in Beith and most of all meeting a historical piece of fabulous silverware. All this of course wouldn't have been possible if they weren't successful in claiming the big prize in that penalty shootout at Rugby Park, and to think I was daft enough to want Beith to lose in the final.

Matchday Stats

Monday 6th June 2016 (7pm ko)

West Region Super League

Beith Juniors 1 (Collins 35) Pollok 1 (Hepburn 49)

Att.180.est

Ground no.528

22. Goodwill City

Bathgate Thistle - Creamery Park (July 2016)

The interlude between one season ending and the next football campaign beginning seemed to get shorter every year. In fact football doesn't end at all if you're a cumulative ardent watcher of the game. This summer we had the Euros, the Europa League qualifying rounds started on the 28th June and there's also women's football throughout the warmer months, although personally I'm not a fan of boilers football!

My final game of last season was the match at Beith on the 6th of June, so only a couple of football blank Saturdays before the "official" start of the 2016-17 season, which begins on the 1st of July. This year I decided to have a proper break from football, no boring pre-season friendlies for me, instead my Saturdays were taking up by other pastimes. I had a few days out at the races, losing plenty of my hard earned on the gee-gees. The 59 U.K. Racecourses is a new list which I'm keen to eventually complete, although this may be a long way off as I've still got fifty left. I had weekends away in Liverpool (my favourite English city) and in Leeds where I saw Belly, one of my favourite bands from the 90s. I even took in a bit of cricket, lending my supporting to my local club Gateshead Fell, so this and all these other days out obviously included the consumption of plenty of ale.

Alas another birthday has come and gone, but my 51st was a special one as it was my son James' 18th birthday. I used my birthday as the starting point of the new season, attending matchday numero uno two days later, on the 27th of July. As I'm aiming to finish this book before the climate changes in late November, I needed to do a double of two nights of games with a stopover in between. The pre-season fixtures aligned nicely with a match at Bathgate on a Wednesday night and Cumnock the following evening. I got the go-ahead to stay with James Little in Edinburgh and as far as work was concerned, Wednesday was my day off and I cashed in a favour for the Thursday, so I was all set to go.

I set off up the A1 at lunchtime, this stretch of motorway is mostly a single carriage, favoured by caravaners and farmers, so I eventually arrived at James' digs at 3.15pm. I didn't even have time for a cuppa, quickly dropping off my bag before scuttling straight off to Waverley Station. Since my last visit to Edinburgh a new Weatherspoon's pub has opened just outside the station called The Booking Office, so we felt obliged to called in for a couple of pints before catching the 1648 to Bathgate.

The train journey to the West Lothian town took 35 minutes, found 5 miles west of Livingston. Bathgate dates to the 12th century, with the first recorded details appearing in a confirmation charter by King Malcolm IV. The name appeared as 'Bathchet' which is an earlier Cumbric name meaning 'Boar Wood'. Historical records reveal that around 1160, the King commanded Uchtred - Sheriff of Linlithgow and Geoffrey de Melville to measure out an area of land which was to form the foundation of Bathgate Parish. The church and all its related property were placed under the auspices of Holyrood Abbey and a tenth of its income from the land was paid to that institution.

Marjorie Bruce (or Marjorie de Brus) was the eldest daughter of Robert the Bruce, and in 1315 she married Walter Stewart, the 6th Lord High Steward of Scotland. The dowry to her husband included the lands and castle of Bathgate. This marriage is still celebrated in an annual pageant, forming part of the Bathgate Procession & John Newlands Festival, now simply known as the Bathgate Gala Day.

The town has a population of around 20,000 and throughout the years there have been many notable residents. Famous people from the town include Scottish obstetrician Sir James Young Simpson who discovered the anaesthetic properties of chloroform, Ryder Cup golf captain Bernard Gallacher (aye! the one with the fit daughter on Sky Sports) and IndyCar champion Dario Franchitti and his young car racing brother Marino. Actor David Tennant was also born in the town before growing up in Paisley. His father was Sandy McDonald, former Moderator of the General Assembly of the Church of Scotland, who in the early 1980s co-presented the Scottish Television religious magazine programme That's the Spirit! The tenth Doctor Who appeared alongside his dad in an episode of the long running Sci-Fi drama in May 2008, making a non-speaking cameo appearance in the episode "The Unicorn and the Wasp".

The band Goodbye Mr Mackenzie, formed in Bathgate in 1984. The Mackenzie's were a popular local rock outfit who released Good Deeds and Dirty Rags on Capitol Records in 1989, their first of four-studio album, which peaked at no.26 in the UK Album Chart. The band had a few hit singles in the Indie Chart but struggled to have a major hit single, with their best seller being 'The Rattler' which sneaked into the Top 40. The band continued to play live until 1995, at which point the young lassie on keyboards - Shirley Manson had gone onto greater things, having major success as the lead singer of Garbage.

On arrival, we took a walk along the main drag to tick off another 'Spoons boozer. The James Young is named in honour of the man who discovered cannel coal in the Boghead area of the town, opening the world's first commercial oil works in 1852, which manufactured paraffin oil and wax. When the cannel coal resources dwindled around 1866, Young started distilling paraffin from much more readily available kerogen shale. The landscape of the Lothians is still dotted with the orange spoil heaps, known as bings, which stems back from this era.

While in the pub I received a message on Twitter from the Bathgate Thistle media guy Robert Allen asking if he could interview me about my travels for Thistle TV, so considering I'm a self-confessed media whore, I more than willingly agreed. When we arrived at Creamery Park we were told to go straight to the clubhouse, no admission taking, giving the special guests star treatment by the club. I met Robert in the clubhouse who introduced me to Robert Napier the club secretary.

We chatted about the club and their Junior Cup success which was obviously heavily featured in the room, with photograph, match worn shirts and winner's medals.

Thistle reached their first Scottish Junior Cup final in 2006, losing 2–1 to Auchinleck Talbot but were triumphant two years later beating Cumnock Juniors 2-1 in the 2008 final with goals from Stevie Menmuir and Paul McGrillen. Menmuir was a very talented centre half who had previously played with Camelon Juniors, while McGrillen had a fine career in the Senior game counting Motherwell, Airdrie and Falkirk amongst his former clubs. The decisive and controversial winning goal came after a smart one-two on the edge of the box with Stephen Docherty, which he stabbed towards goal. The keeper managed to get a touch onto it, taking all the pace off it, but it managed to squirm over the line – much to the Cumnock defenders frustrations. It was a close call but it definitely crossed over for a goal according to the Thistle fans, however the Cumnock defenders furiously protested to the ref that the ball hadn't fully crossed over the line. To this day, the Cumnock fans still believe it shouldn't have counted whereas over the years the Jags fans claim it was over by miles.

Match winner and Man of the Match Paul McGrillen life ended in tragedy, sadly, Paul was found hanged in July 2009 at his home. Paul was still playing for Bathgate Thistle at the time and the circumstances remain a mystery. A match is held most years between Bathgate Thistle and Motherwell in memory of Paul and he is sadly missed by everyone involved with the club.

Football in the town goes way back, with a record of an organised match dating as far back as April 1849 when the local Courier newspaper reported, "A match took place on the ground of the Bathgate Club between Clarkson and the home team when victory fell to the strangers by four goals to none". The game took off within the town with several clubs formed, including Bathgate Athletic, The Volunteers, Durhamtown Rangers, West Lothian Thistle and Bathgate Rovers. In July 1893, Bathgate Football Club formed, following a public meeting which was held to pull resources and focus on one club within the town. The senior side went onto play in the Scottish League when the new Second Division was founded in 1921. The town switched to the Junior ranks in 1936 when Bathgate Thistle Junior Football Club was formed, taking up the vacancy in the Midlothian League for the 1938/39 season.

The new club took up residence at Creamery Park next to the Co-operative Creamery in Hardhill Road. Nowadays the ground has a large standing terrace down one side, which was opened in 2012, with the other three sides are made up of grass banking. Beside the stand is a relatively new building, housing the changing rooms, clubhouse and refreshment bar. A special feature of the ground is the immaculate pitch, which isn't just the best in the Juniors leagues, but probably one of the best in Scotland. The groundsman also works at Ratho Park Golf Club and takes pride in the Creamery Park pitch, affectionately calling it "his baby"

The club was revamped in the Spring of 2013, incorporating existing local Amateur, youth and children teams to become Bathgate Thistle Community FC. They currently play in the East Region Premier League following their relegation from the Superleague in 2012.

Thistle were up against Super League side Hill of Beath Hawthorn in a pre-season friendly on a pleasant warm summers evening. After a pretty poor start the match finally sparked into life just before half time, when the ball dropped to Aaron Hay on the edge of the box, to fire in on the half volley.

During the interval, I met Robert back in the clubhouse and after a fresh cup of tea straight out of the pot and some laid on snacks, I did the piece for the website. I was fearful of how the interview would come across, but after watching it back I was chuffed with it and it's now available for the world to viddy on YouTube (just put in the obvious search of ... Thistle TV - Shaun Smith) Rob also told us the team are currently struggling with injuries, especially in defence nodding towards their 54 cap Gambian centre-half Hassan Nyang who was sitting in the clubhouse. I didn't want to ask how an experienced international from the west coast of northern Africa ended up Bathgate, but it's one hell of a coup!

The second period saw a vast improvement with Thistle making a promising start until the visitors took control, with Lee Reid heading in a right-wing cross on 53 minutes. Haws substitute Callum Reid wrapped the game up, with a strong run and powerful shot which spun in off the unlucky 'keeper, before showing good composure to make it 4-0 with twenty minutes remaining.

Although the match wasn't a classic it was good to get my new season underway and more importantly back on the Scottish Joons trail, the evening made that bit more special by the warm reception on a warm night (including get in for nowt) received by the two Roberts at Bathgate Thistle.

Matchday Stats

Wednesday 27th July 2016

Pre-Season Friendly

Bathgate Thistle 0

Hill of Beath Hawthorn 4(hay 43 L.Reid 53 C.Reid 67,70)

Att.110hc   Ground no.529

23. Black and White Unite

Cumnock Juniors - Townhead Park (July 2016)

 After last night's game at Bathgate, it was an early start the following morning. The indignant pain of being a resident in Edinburgh is having to obtain a permit to park outside your own property, so non-permit holders must pay, allowed just a maximum of 4 hours during none peak times. This meant I had to check out of Little Towers at 9.45am, but not before he cooked me a lovely hearty breakfast, not just for myself but also his other house guests, as his pal Ronnie and his family were staying for their annual trip from Hong Kong. I said my goodbyes then drove down to Cameron Toll Retail Park to take advantage of the free car parking, so I could spend the day in the capital.

It was a refreshing change to take a nice stroll around the city and spend more time record shop digging. I picked up an early and quite rare Throwing Muses album, plus an immaculate copy of The Cost of Loving by The Style Council. This certainly won't go down as Weller's finest moment on plastic, in fact it's horrendous in some parts and probably the worst album he's ever recorded. Even so I just had to buy it, because I've got all their other albums, so my OCD kicked in meaning I needed to purchase it for the full set.

After a pleasant day, where due to Scottish drinking laws I resisted calling into one of the city's fine hostelries, I returned to the car at 3 o'clock. I set off along the City of Edinburgh Bypass, then exiting onto the A71 Kilmarnock Road towards Ayrshire. Whilst on route I was thinking that at some point I must stop for a break and a nanna nap. I wasn't particularly tired, but I knew I'd be feeling weary on the drive home, and I didn't want to risk being found abandoned in a ditch somewhere along the A69 later that night.

When I reached the M74 it was a quick ten-minute drive down to the junction for the A70 and conveniently there was the Cairn Lodge services, so I pulled up in the car park, climbed into the back seat for a forty-minute kip. After a refreshing coffee, I went about tackling the slender country Ayr Road to Cumnock.

I arrived in Cumnock an hour before the kick off, allowing plenty of time for a wander around the town which lies at the confluence of both the Lugar and Glaisnock Waters. The name of the town has been disputed throughout its history, with a few different interpretations such as Com-cnoc, (hollow of the hills) Cam-cnoc, (crooked hill) Com-oich, (meeting of the waters) and Cumanag, (little shrine).

The area has seen human settlement for over 5,000 years, with many Bronze Age burial sites around the nearby area. Cumnock's Square is believed to have been a place of worship since the 10th century, though the earliest records begin in about 1275. The centre of the town is home to the magnificent Old Church which was built in 1867 and the Mercat Cross, which dates to 1703, which is featured on the football club badge.

Cumnock has a strong industrial history and social heritage, housing many miners, serving as the market town for the smaller neighbouring towns like New Cumnock, Lugar, Auchinleck, Muirkirk and Ochiltree. The founder of the Scottish Labour Party and their first MP, James Keir Hardie worked as a journalist in Cumnock and

I took a picture for Instagram of the striking bust of Hardie, found at the front entrance of the town hall.

As it was tea time I had a tobby around in search for something to eat. I really fancied some fish & chips but couldn't find a chippy, although I wouldn't be stuck if I was in the mood for a kebab with a few rotisseries on show, but who fancies a kebab without at least necking half a dozen pints first? As I approached Townhead Park from the town centre I noticed a large queue snaking out of a doorway opposite, and so it was here I discovered Nellos chippy. After eventually reaching the front of the queue I recalled having to ask for a fish supper, as the word "supper" north of the border is a substitute word for "and chips" and not a dish to consume just before bedtime.

I arranged to meet up with Graham Crofts from the 100 grounds Club and his daughter Lois at the game, who had travelled up from Dumfries to watch their beloved Doonhamers. As we entered the turnstiles I asked about programme and badges, but unfortunately neither was available. During the first half I was approached by Tom Bradford, the guy on the gate, who knowing I was a stranger, invite me up into the boardroom at half time for a cup of tea. I told him about the book so he showed me around the boardroom and we discussed the history of the club, who were formed back in 1912. The Noch have won the Scottish Junior Cup twice beating Bo'ness United 1-0 in 1979 with a goal by Jimmy Flynn and a decade late they defeated Ormiston Primrose by the same score, with Derek Love bagging the winner. They have also finished runners-up twice losing out to Blantyre Vics in 1950 and last night's visited club Bathgate Thistle, which I cheekily mentioned and past on their regards from the previous evening. Not surprisingly that contentious was it over the line or not winning goal was mentioned during the conversation. Throughout the years, they've been Ayrshire League champions on 11 occasions and more recently the Super League Division One in 2015-16. Cup honours include 7 Ayrshire Cup wins, the Ayrshire District Cup on four occasions and the Ayrshire League Cup 15 times.

I would have loved my visit to Townhead Park to have coincided with a match against Auchinleck Talbot. I've heard plenty of tales about the rivalry between the two clubs on my travels, with the fixture tagged the "Old Firm" of Junior football due to the avid support from both clubs. Crowds of around 6,000 was a regular occurrence during the 1970s and 80s, with a Junior Cup tie attracting well over 8,000 during this era.

Tom introduced me to the Club President Wullie McVake, Vice President Wullie Dick and Secretary George Morton and a few others, one of which had played for Sheffield United and was an MBE, although I don't know if they were just having me on or if the canny ex-player had actually met Her Majesty. They were keen to give me a souvenir of my visit so they looked around for a gift, Wullie McVake asked if a match worn football shirt would be ok, adding that it's black & white stripes, as if this would make a difference to whether I would want it or not. As you can imagine my little face lit up and I gleefully accepted the jersey, they also took my address and promised to send me some programmes and a badge when they come to hand. When I went back outside assistant secretary Neil Robertson collared me to make sure they had my address, so once again the kindness and hospitality shown by the host clubs during this project has been second to none.

Townhead Park has undergone a fair bit work during the spring, with a new all-weather pitch installed which meant home matches were played up the road in Lugar. The 3,000-capacity ground has a covered enclosure down one side behind the dugouts. At the far goal is another covered terrace which has a fabulous mural on the back wall covering the club's past glories. The changing rooms, boardroom, hospitality and the Nock Nosh food cabin are all housed in one building behind the turnstile entrance goal.

As for the match, Cumnock looked a decent outfit and could be in for a good season judging by their display against a youthful Queen of the South side. They bossed the match, carving out a string of good chances until finally taking the lead on 65 minutes, when Shirkie picked up the ball on the edge of the box and fired in low hard drive. They doubled the lead on 78 minutes with a fabulous individual effort (and early contender for my 16-17 Goal of my Season) from Keir Samson, who took the ball down on his chest, turned the defender and volleyed in a looping shot into the far corner. After saying my farewells to Graham and Lois, I took a slow walk towards the exit when I saw Shirkie grab his second goal of the night, netting the rebound after the 'keeper pulled off a good save from distance to make it 3-0 in the dying moments.

After the match, I rushed straight off, aiming to get on the M74 before it got too dark. The wet weather and poor visibility made the drive home hard work at times, but I still made decent time to get home just before midnight. (before I turn into a pumpkin)

During this process, I've always thought I would fall for a club and adopt them as my Junior team. I've really enjoyed visited most the clubs, so there' a lot of candidates so far along the journey, but Cumnock Juniors are right up there and I have the black and white jersey to prove it.

Matchday Stats

Thursday 28th July 2016 (7pm ko)

Pre-Season Friendly

Cumnock Juniors 3 (Shirkie 65, 89 Samson 78)

Queen of the South U-20 0

Att.200.est

Ground no.530

24.King of the Castle

Blantyre Victoria - Castle Park (August 2016)

On the 16th May 1970, a young laddie travelled over from Edinburgh for his first visit to the national stadium, to see his favourite Junior team Penicuik Athletic face Blantyre Victoria in the final of the Scottish Junior Cup. He travelled by car with Hugh Old, a friend of his dad who managed to get them some decent seats in the old stand. Hugh ran the local amateur side Dalmore United and a couple of their players filled the car, all anticipating the Rookie Cookie bringing the Holy Grail back to Midlothian.

The 19,500 in attendance saw the teams share a goal apiece in a tight affair which meant they had to do it all over again on the following Tuesday night. The young teenager wasn't allowed to attend the replay, as his Mum wasn't keen on him going to Glasgow on a school night, however Hugh persuaded her to let him go as it might be the only time Penicuik would ever get to the final.

The replay was a huge disappointment for the Penicuik supporters as another goal from Jim Lynn was good enough to see The Vics lift the old trophy in front of a crowd of 14,225. Hugh was correct with his prophecy too, as Penicuik haven't reach the final since and as for the young lad in question, well that's someone you already know, as it was my fellow travelling companion James Little.

As he's seen them win the trophy it was only right for both of us to pay our first visit to Castle Park together. The pain in the backside, but understandably essential engineering works on the East Coast line meant I had to take the Cumbrian train route to Glasgow. I boarded the 0824 to Carlisle then after a quick train swap I was enjoying a pint in the Sir John Moore by half past eleven. At the bar, I met up with Mark Wilkins who had travelled up from London to take in the match at Arthurlie, before nipping back to the station for the 1206 Hamilton bound service to Blantyre.

The civil parish in South Lanarkshire is a short 20-minute train journey, just 8 miles south-east of Glasgow. The town has a population of about 17,500, its name deriving from Cumbric origins - blaen tir which translates as "top of the land" with the earliest settlement dating back to the Bronze Age in the small hamlet of High Blantyre.

The town is bounded by four stretches of water with the River Clyde to the north, the Rotten Burn to the south, the Park Burn to the east and the Rotten Calder to the west.

The area was a centre for large manufacturing of cotton-related products during the 18th century, before becoming heavily involved in coal mining during the 19th and 20th centuries. In October 1877, the town was the site of the Blantyre Mining Disaster when 207 miners died in an explosion at William Pit numbers 1 and 2, the youngest being an 11-year-old boy. A monument to the disaster sits at the High Blantyre Cross and there's an annual march to commemorate the tragedy. The traditional song 'The Blantyre Explosion' was recorded by amongst others Christy Moore and Luke Kelly, the touching lyrics beautifully sum up the events of that fateful day on the 22nd of October.

Blantyre's most famous son is the 19th century missionary and explorer David Livingstone, who was born at Shuttle Row in 1813. The town has the David Livingstone Centre, located in the mill building house where he was born. The museum is next to the iron suspension bridge which runs over the Clyde into Bothwell, where the ruins of Blantyre Priory stand opposite Bothwell Castle.

I met James at the station, as his train from Edinburgh arrived just a few minutes earlier. We had plenty of time for a drink before the 2 o'clock kick-off, so we ventured into a couple of the local pubs. I usually look online for any decent boozers before heading off on my travels, but nothing outstanding came to light, so we decided to just take pot luck. After coming out of Station Road we took a right turn onto the main Glasgow Road, where we stumbled upon The Old Original Bar. As we walked in we were greeted with suspicion, with the half a dozen customers thinking we were a couple of strangers in search of the Rangers v Hamilton lunchtime kick off game on TV. A couple of young lads were sitting next to the door and asked me if I was here to watch Rangers, I replied "No, I'm here to watch Blantyre" which prompted one of them to stand up, spread his arms in the quarter to three pose and shout at the top of his voice - "This is F**king Blantyre"

As you can imagine we consumed our pints swiftly and looked for an alternative watering hole on route to the ground. The next pub we came across was the Stonefield Tavern, which didn't look too bad from the outside, so we were taking aback when we got inside to discover it was actually a Rangers bar, with the pub decorated with an array of club jerseys and memorabilia. There were no clues from the exterior that this was a Gers boozer, so any random stranger wearing the wrong football attire could have mistakenly strolled in, however unlike the last bar, there was no Rangers game on the box.

We decided not to bother looking for another pub instead we headed to the ground. Castle Park has obviously seen better days but it's discrepancies give it plenty of character. There is a standing cover on the far side, where some of the roof is missing and terracing behind the Forrest Street goal, with the canteen near the corner flag. There's wooden sleepers which are used for seats in front of the central changing rooms, although you must be careful to not get splinters in your backside.

Blantyre Victoria are one of the oldest clubs in Lanarkshire, founded in 1890, winning the first of six Lanarkshire League titles in 1892–93. The Vics played in their first Junior Cup final in 1944, narrowly losing 1-0 to Perthshire, but since then they've won the trophy on three occasions. In 1950 they beat Cumnock 3-0, then 20 years later came that victory over Penicuik Athletic. The Junior Cup hat-trick came in 1982 with a single goal victory over Baillieston, but since completing a hat-trick of Junior Cup titles the cup honours have tried up, although they have won a few lower league titles. In 2013-14 they lifted the Central League Division 2, then the Division 1 title the following season, so they're now in the West of Scotland Superleague First Division.

The club shared a healthy rivalry with Blantyre Celtic, who were formed in 1914 originally as Blantyre United. The club played in the Springwell end of the town and reached the Junior Cup semi-finals in 1924, 1938 and 1946, but lost on each occasion. The club dissolved in 1992 and amongst their former players was renowned Celtic winger Jimmy Johnstone, however the Vics out trump their old rivals, as

the hoops legendary manager Jock Stein, former skipper
Billy McNeil, as well as Scottish international striker Joe
Jordan have all reigned as kings of Castle Park.

Blantyre were up against Vale of Clyde in the opening
group stage game of the Central Sectional League Cup. The
Vale got off to a fabulous start when they were awarded a
penalty with just 24 seconds gone, which was confidently
converted by James McKinstry. The referee was
persecuted for the next 89 minutes from the Vics
supporters and the home dugout because of that early
penalty decision, but they levelled things up on 25 minutes
when a good left wing cross was headed home by Jack
Marriot. The Vics sporting their blue and white striped
shirts looked on course for victory when Ross Smith
latched onto a neat through ball to round the keeper and
score, but that lead lasted just five minutes when a ball
from the left flank was nodded in at the far post by Scott
McManus on 78 minutes. The game could have gone either
way, but with just three minutes remaining a peach of a
cross by McKinstry was headed home by Stephen Gray to
grab the three points for Vale of Clyde.

We both enjoyed our visit to Blantyre and an entertaining
match at Castle Park, which resulted in a 3-2 defeat for
home side, but unfortunately as far as James is concerned,
seeing The Vics defeated came 46 years too late. After
saying farewell to James I caught the 1618 train but
alighted at Rutherglen for a drink, before continuing the
rest of the journey to Glasgow Central for the 1800 to
Carlisle, eventually arriving back on Tyneside around 9
o'clock.

Matchday Stats

<u>Saturday 6th August 2016 (2pm ko)</u>

Exsel Group Central Sectional League Cup – Group Stage (Section 4)

Blantyre Victoria 2(Marriot 25 Smith 73)

Vale of Clyde 3(McKinstry 2pen McManus 78 Gray 87)

Ground no.537

25.Why Does It Always Rain on Me?

Whitburn Junior - Central Park (August 2016)

There's indisputably nothing worse in this Groundhopping hobby than looking forward to a game at a new ground, only to find on arrival that the match is off. This has happened a few times during my football travelling career but the worst of them all came in December 2002, when I jetted down to Barcelona with the Toon Army, full of excitement in anticipation for our Champions League Second Phase clash in the Camp Nou.

When we arrived, it was a typical Spanish sunny day, however I did notice a few puddles outside Barca Airport, so I thought there must've been a few rain showers overnight. It wasn't until much later that afternoon that we found out that there had been torrential rain over the last few days and the match was in doubt. A further deluge a few hours before kick-off meant the match was off, so I'd wasting a day off work and even worse found myself a few hundred quid out of pocket. This was the daddy of all postponements and certainly the biggest kick in the ball bag I've ever had in attempting to attend a football match. The fact I got as far as the Camp Nou exterior gates but was denied the chance of watching a match, had been a monkey on my back that I finally tossed aside during the writing of this book when I saw Barca while on holiday in Salou.

Back in January I went against my vow of not returning to Scotland until the Spring by arranged a road trip to Whitburn with the "North-East Celebrity Groundhopping Couple" I know around this time of year matches are more likely to be postponed but I just couldn't help myself, I was desperate to mark another one off the list.

Lee and Katie arrived at my house at 8.15 on the Saturday morning, from where I was driving straight up to Livingston, to tick off the two Wetherspoon's pubs in the town centre precinct, have breakfast, and from here we'd find out if the Whitburn game was on. If it was postponed then it was a further one hour drive to Barrhead for the Arthurlie game, which was our backup option. If that match also fell foul to the weather then we had a third option as Alloa were at home and guaranteed to go ahead because of their all-weather surface, so whatever the outcome we knew we would be going to a game somewhere. As we sat enjoying our fry ups in Livi I was delighted to learn that Whitburn's match opponents Blackburn United, had confirmed the pitch had passed its 9.30am inspection. The good news was confirmed when Robert, who does the Twitter feed for Whitburn, confidently posted pictures of Central Park looking in great nick.

We left Livingston and took a leisurely eight-mile drive along to Whitburn, arrived just outside the ground half an hour before the 1.45pm kick off. I had just got out of the car when I was approached by a bloke retrieving a stray football from the nearby street, who asked if I was here for the match before adding that it's just been called off. Coincidentally the gentleman that broke the news was Robert who I had earlier contacted on Twitter. He knew who I was and how far I had travelled, so he felt bad having to inform me that although the local referee passed the pitch earlier, when the match ref arrived he wasn't happy with a soft patch in and around the corner flag of around 5 square metres, which he deemed unsafe for the players. How can two referees have opposite opinions on a wee patch of grass? The match referee should have done the morning inspection, but when he arrived at the ground he obviously wasn't in the mood to run around a football pitch for an hour and a half, when you consider it was a bright dry day with no rain forecast. The fact they were playing Blackburn, a club based just two and a half miles away, meant it was an easy decision to call it off. If they were playing a Junior Cup tie against a club with a large travelling support, I would bet a large wedge of cash that the referee would tell the groundsman to chuck a few buckets of sand on the damp patch and it would be game on.

I remembered the previous evening when I was looking at the East Region fixtures, vaguely recollected that Fauldhouse were at home and I knew it was somewhere near Whitburn. I asked Robert where it was and he told me it was about 7 minutes away and gave me precise directions to their ground. So, we raced up the hill towards Longridge, then a sharp left along to Fauldhouse, so we arrived a good ten minutes before kick-off. We didn't have any idea who they were playing, so we entered the ground and saw there was already a decent crowd gathering as the Hoose were hosting Bo'ness United. We saw a decent match with the away team recording a 5-2 victory which I enjoyed, but deep inside I was really peeved off with missing out on one off my list.

Fast forward to the summer and the eve of the 2016-17 season, as I studied the fixtures for the opening month of the season. One fixture that caught my eye was a West Lothian midweek derby between Whitburn Junior and Bathgate Thistle. The kick off was at 7 o'clock so I contacted Lee and Katie a few weeks in advance to ask them to keep that night free, so we could have another crack at ticking off Central Park. On this occasion, we departed at 2.45pm, taking a different route by avoiding the A1 and instead driving across the picturesque A68. When we reached the border crossing at Carter Bar we stopped for a refreshment break, stopping for a cup of coffee while my passengers had an ice cream. Katie also purchased a teddy bear from one of the souvenir traders, who take advantage of passing tourists by selling fluffy toys decorated in tartan. The drive onwards to West Lothian was nicely timed, arriving once again half an hour before the game. This leg of the journey was mostly spent trying to give Katie's new woolly friend a name, with my suggestion of "Burnie" being the best and most obvious choice.

Whitburn takes its name from Scottish Gaelic, meaning 'The White Burn' The town currently has a population of over 10,000, which was boosted by the Glasgow overflow during the 1960s. The nearby Polkemmet Colliery was one of Scotland's most important pits, providing a large workforce and a major supplier of coking coal to the Ravenscraig Steelworks in Motherwell. The mine closed in controversial circumstances because of damage caused by flooding, occurring during the 1984-85 miners' strike. After its closure, persistent spontaneous combustion problems in the bing generated noxious fumes meant when the wind blew a certain way the smell was instantly recognisable to regular travellers on the passing M8 motorway.

Before the match, we had enough time for a chippy tea, calling into Tony's on East Main Street. I enjoying the unknown delicacy of a palatable King Rib Supper, while Katie was keen to know what was in the brown stuff in the clear plastic vinegar bottles. The staff in the chippy were shocked that she didn't know of the famous Scottish delicacy of Chippie Sauce, which is basically brown sauce mixed with vinegar. Katie and Lee both liked it so much, she bought a bottle to take home. We arranged to meet with James Little so he joined us as we dined at the picnic table in Central Park, but this isn't New York, but a table and chair set next to the turnstile entrance inside another football ground.

The ground was built during the early 1930s and is dominated by a large covered wooden sleeper terrace on the far side which runs almost pitch length. The enclosure came from an old Polish army camp on the Polkemmet estate and was erected in 1946. The rest of the ground is made up of grass banking behind each goal and a section of paddock terracing. The changing rooms are at the entrance side next to the impressive social club, which has a quite homely ambience and as you could imagine a fine collection of club memorabilia.

When I started this quest, I knew that Whitburn would have to be done at a later stage, as the pavilion roof was blown off in December 2013. The club relocated to Whitburn Academy and finally returning home after work on the changing rooms was completed in October 2015.

The football club came together in 1934, originating from Whitburn Amateurs who formed the previous decade. The old amateur side wore a blue and white strip, the kit donated by local bookie Bob Gray, which set him back the grand sum of a tenner. The club switching to the Junior ranks to seek entry into the East of Scotland Junior League, following a meeting at Baillie Institute in January 1934. During the following six months, several fundraising events took place by the newly formed supporters club to get the new Junior side up and running. Whitburn finally played their first match on the 28th July against another new club Musselburgh Athletic in the Midlothian League. The Whitburn Public Band provided pre-match and half time entertainment, with the match finishing 2-2, enjoyed by a crowd of around 700.

The club switched to the Motherwell style colours of amber and claret, winning their first pieces of silverware after the war, achieving the double of the St Michael's Cup and the Edinburgh League Cup in 1946-47. The club were then starved of success until another cup double during the 1959-60 season, with the Brown Cup and RL Rea Cup residing at Central Park. Throughout their history there's been the odd trophy success in the likes of the Fife & Lothian Cup and East of Scotland Cup, however the club's most successful period came after winning the East Region Division One title for the first time in 1985-86. They were champions on another half a dozen occasions, the last of which came in season 2000-01, when they also claimed their fifth Brown Cup success.

The Burnie were twice runners up in the Scottish Junior Cup, suffering that heavy replay defeat to Bonnyrigg Rose in 1966 and losing the 1995 final 2-0 to Camelon. They lifted the trophy at the third attempt becoming the first winners of the 21st century, beating Johnstone Burgh at Firhill Stadium. The match finished all square, with a penalty from Callum Milne and a Colin L. Campbell header making it 2-2 after 90 minutes. The sides still weren't separated after extra time, so for the first time in the history of the Scottish Junior Cup, the 6,547 in attendance were to witness the final decided by a penalty shootout.

Johnstone went first, with Lindsay scoring easily, as did Callum Milne with Whitburn's first kick. Burnie keeper Rab Burns made a fine save to deny Lee Martin, however that advantage didn't last long as Paul Taylor saw his effort saved. Both teams were successful with their next two kicks, Connie and Millar for Johnstone, with Gilmour and Clouston scoring for Whitburn to make it 3-3 with one kick each left.

With the pressure on, Johnstone's McGuire fired his spot-kick wide, which left Whitburn skipper Stevie Prior with the golden chance to win the cup for his team. Stevie took a long run up and although 'keeper Donahoe managed to get his fingers to the ball, the powerful shot found the back of the net and at long last, their name on the famous old trophy.

The club were regular challengers in East Region Superleague from 2002, but since their relegation in 2010 they haven't returned to the top division. Last season they won promotion from the East Region South Division along with Tranent Juniors, so they are on their way back up currently sitting in the East Premier League.

Central Park was quite a stunning setting on this warm summers evening. The match saw a late equaliser from Callum Robertson rescued a point for the Burnie against ten-man Thistle. After seeing Bathgate just a few weeks earlier, they looked a much better side showing a vast improvement. They took a 16th minute lead when a lob from Robbie Feeney just managed to find the net after the 'keeper failed to claw out his 20-yard effort, and they could have easily extended their advantage after a promising start to the game.

Just before the break the visitors were reduced to ten men after a late challenge from Darren McIntosh on Taylor, with the defender shown a straight red card. Despite being a man down they looked on course to take the three points until Robertson headed home a left-wing cross on 82 minutes. Both sides went full pelt in the last ten minutes looking for a winner and Whitburn looked to have clinched it, but Robertson's effort was chalked off by the unpopular referee for offside. The Jags famous Gambian international centre-half must still be out injured, as he was on the side-lines with his mobile phone constantly glued to his ear. We reckoned that maybe he wasn't injured at all but out of favour and on the phone to his agent looking for a move out of Bathgate!

This was the last set of midweek fixtures until the spring, so the drive north after work was well worth it, when you consider the quiet traffic back along the M8 and down the A1, which meant I was back home for 11.20pm.

Matchday Stats

Wednesday 17th August (6.45pm ko)

East Region Premier League

Whitburn Junior 1(Robertson 82)

Bathgate Thistle 1(Feeney 16)

Att.200est   Ground no.538

26. Head On

East Kilbride Thistle - The Show Park

(September 2016)

I left school just short of my sixteenth birthday, having accumulated seven GCSEs, all average to poor grades in subjects that wouldn't contribute to my adult working life. Since I started researching my football destinations I've gathered lots of historical facts and the odd piece of pointless information. Take what I've learned about East Kilbride for example - A small village in the central belt of Scotland, which took its name from an Irish saint and with less than one thousand inhabitants increased from a wee village into the largest satellite town in South Lanarkshire.

My only previous knowledge of East Kilbride was it being the birthplace of two brothers who after being inspired by punk, formed The Jesus & Mary Chain in 1983. To understate that Jim and William Reid are siblings that "don't really get on with each other" is putting it politely, in fact their relationship is so dreadful they make the Gallagher brothers from Oasis look like *The Waltons*.

During their early days, they performed amphetamine fuelled short gigs in small venues, playing with their backs to the audience and refusing to speak. During a gig in December 1984 bottles were thrown on the stage, with the press dramatizing events claiming there had been a riot. That national rag which is named after the largest star in the sky, ran a story focusing on the drugs and violence, giving the band the tag of "The new Sex Pistols" Just like the Pistols eight years earlier, the bad press led to several councils banning the band from playing in their region. As far as the music business is concerned there's no such thing as a bad press, as the band went from strength to strength, releasing half a dozen successful albums and a string of hit singles.

In 2007 the Mary Chain reformed playing live shows and I saw the band for the first time in over 20 years in February 2015, when they performed their debut album *Psychocandy* in full. They were just as loud as when I saw them back in their heyday, playing with an immense frenzy of guitar feedback, so much so that my ears felt like they were bleeding from the sheer white noise.

East Kilbride lies on high ground on the south side of the Cathkin Braes, about 8 miles southeast of Glasgow, enclosed by the White Cart River to the west and the Rotten Calder to the east, which flows northwards to join the Clyde.

The name derives from St Brigit, who founded a monastery for nuns and monks in Kildare, Ireland in the 6th century. In turn Dál Riatan monks introduced her order to Scotland. The association with the saint originates from the first parish church which was located on the site of a pre-Christian sacred well, dedicated to the Celtic goddess Brigid.

East Kilbride was just a small village with around 900 inhabitants in 1930. The lack of housing in Glasgow following the Second World War, plus a large working population throughout Scotland's Central Belt meant this was the perfect location for the country's first new town in May 1947. The town centre is a large shopping mall surrounded by subdivided residential precincts, in which each area has its own shops, primary schools and community facilities, with a growing population of almost 75,000.

My pal from work Honest Paul joined me on this occasion, as he was keen to accompany me on another of my trips following a cracking day out last season when we went to Cambuslang Rangers. We reached Glasgow Central train station at 11.15, having travelled via the Carlisle route, then quickly scuttled down to the Sir John Moore on Argyle Street for breakfast. Paul is a vegetarian, mainly due to the preaching's of Morrissey, so every time we've had a 'Spoons breakfast together he always questions the sausages, suspicious that they may contain meat. We also met Mark Wilkins in the pub for a drink, he had travelled up from Euston, so he met us for a quick pint before the three of us went our separate ways. Paul had brought a wedge of cash with him as he wanted to have a tobby around Glasgow to do some retail therapy, while Mark headed to Wishaw Juniors as he's already been to East Kilbride Thistle. I caught the 1218 train, the journey taking about half an hour, so I had time to walk to the centre for a pint in the Hay Stock before the 2 o'clock start, via under one of the many large roundabouts which splits the town into its different areas. I arrived at the Showpark around 20 minutes before kick-off, so plenty of time to take some photos and have a good look around before the game, however my latest Joons appearance didn't get off to the best of starts. Outside the turnstile entrance there's a car park with a sign on the ground's perimeter wall which states 'Welcome to the Show Park'. As I was taking a picture of the sign I heard a few blokes shouting at someone. I looked towards the direction of the bawling and noticed two club officials looking in my direction and realised they were shouting at me. One was a tall fellow with a baldy nappa and a grey goatee beard, not the kind of bloke I'd want to get into a scrap with mind. The other was a smaller guy wearing a shirt and tie under his black overcoat.

"What's wrong like?" I shouted back as I took one more picture before walking towards them to find out what their beef was.

"What do you think you're up to?" the big bloke said.

"That's no way to welcome someone who is actually writing a book about you. All I'm doing is taking a few pictures. Your supposed to say something like ...hello! . welcome to the Show Park"

They apologised for the mix up, they thought I was up to some dodgy business with the parked vehicles as they've had a bit bother with damage in the car park recently. I paid my admission, bought the fabulously titled The Jags Mag matchday programme, purchasing a golden goal ticket and had a quick chat with the lads. I later found out that the big bloke was club secretary Peter Kelsall, who finished our conversation with the parting shot of "Oh by the way ...Welcome to the Show Park!"

The 2,300-capacity ground has one main stand which is filled with school type chairs, although the enclosure is mostly redundant as this view is blocked with containers and is set too far back from the pitch. The team dugouts are over the far side, with most of the ground made up of grass banking.

In comparison to other Junior clubs, East Kilbride Thistle are mere young ones formed during my lifetime in 1968.

The Jags won their first piece of silverware in the West of Scotland Cup in 1974, followed by a four trophy haul the following year included winning the Central League A Division for the first time.

Thistle's great Junior Cup achievement came in 1983 when they beat Bo'ness United 2-0 at Ibrox Stadium, with goals from skipper Joe Reilly and Kenny Gordon. This successful era when they also won a fourth league title, as well the Evening Times Trophy and Central Section League Cup ended abruptly. It was another 20 years before they would again be amongst the medals, lifted their third Section Cup in 2002-03.

In 2008 The Jags also launched their own youth development structure, with coaching for boys and girls teams at all age levels from under 4's up to under 21's wearing the classic black and white striped jerseys. The club are currently in the Central District Second Division, since their relegation into the fourth level of the West Region in 2013.

Amongst their former players is Willie Pettigrew who signed for the Jags from Hibernian in 1971. During his short spell at the club he was capped at Junior level and won 5 caps at senior level when he signed for Motherwell, his hometown club in 1972. Pettigrew scored in his first two international appearances and Scotland won all five matches that he played in.

The fixture with Carluke Rovers was only the second league game of the season for both sides. The match was a cracker with the score poised at twos each after only 24 minutes. The lively Carluke striker Ian Watt twice give his side the lead in the first half, but The Jags pegged them back with a fabulous volley from man of the match Phil McCabe and Andy Gibson making it all square.

The second half was terrific end to end stuff with the decisive goal coming from Andy McFadden, who finished off a breakaway move with a curled effort from the left into the far corner. An entertaining encounter which I thoroughly enjoyed and full marks to both teams for going shit or bust throughout the whole ninety minutes.

After the game, I ran all the way to the train station to catch the 1555 back to Glasgow, as I had a pint of Bitter & Twisted with my name on it waiting for me in The Horseshoe Bar. As I was running full pelt a few intrusive local youths tried to slow me down but I made the train with seconds to spare. This got me thinking of earlier in the day when I had to dodge past a bunch of blokes in their forties and fifties drinking cans of cheap lager under the roundabout as I headed into the centre. These minor incidents meant I could fully understand my suspicious arrival at the ground from the good folk at the football club.

I met back up with Paul in the pub, who had my pint waiting and was proudly holding a betting slip, not with a winning horse on it but the phone number of a barmaid he had chatted up in one of the bars earlier in the afternoon. Mark soon joining us for a few drinks, before I introduced Paul to the fabulous Laurieston bar on Bridge Street. I really like this pub, its full of character and full of characters, so we stayed there for a while before we caught the train to Carlisle. We had plenty of time to call into four lively pubs in the town before catching the last train back to Newcastle at 2128.

Another enjoyable day out and now there's just two clubs left on my Scottish Junior odyssey at Irvine Meadow and Arthurlie. So far, I've had the full support of the fixture gods, but with just two grounds left the odds of one being at home on the 1st and another on the 27th of October must be in my favour. I'll just have to keep my fingers, toes and whatever else crossed that fate is again on my side and I bag both these clubs on schedule.

Matchday Stats

Saturday 3rd September (2pm ko)

Central District 2nd Division

East Kilbride Thistle 3(McCabe 13 Gibson 24 McFadden 65)

Carluke Rovers 2(Watt 4,18)

Att.64hc

Ground no.543

27. Let Mother Nature Be Your Guide

Irvine Meadow - Meadow Park (October 2016)

What is the foremost thing you would normally do when returning home from your holidays? Obviously apart from putting the kettle on to make a decent brew, you would more than likely check your mail, unpack the luggage or in my part of the world change into some warmer clothes. After a week away on the Costa Dorada (where I saw four games including one in Camp Nou) I arrived home and logged straight onto the SJFA West Region website to check the fresh round of fixtures. My next work free weekend was the following Saturday, but with having just two grounds remaining I didn't book advanced train tickets in case neither club were down for a home game.

The gentlemen on the fixture committee were kind enough to give me an option with both Arthurlie and Irvine Meadow handed home games, but the question was - which one do I choose? The next Joons trip is four weeks away on the 29th of October, when my mates are joining me in Glasgow for a double celebration of my best pal Zippy's birthday and what I forecasted as the "From the Toon to the Scottish Joons Finale Party" As Arthurlie is closer to Glasgow Central station than Irvine, and not wanting to deny the lads valuable beer bar time, I chose the furthest one away. There was also the adding attraction of the game itself, as Irvine Meadow were up against local rivals Irvine Victoria in the Super League First Division.

The two clubs have already met this season at Meadow Park, in the Section League Cup back in August. The hosts came out on top in a seven-goal thriller in the traditional Marymass Derby. The Marymass Festival has been celebrated since the middle ages and is recognised locally and nationally as a major annual event, which attracts thousands of visitors to Irvine during a 12-day period in mid-August. Deriving from an historic medieval religious festival and local horse fair, it comprises of several events, including one of the UK's longest-running Folk Music Festivals and the Crowning of the Marymass Queen, in honour of the visit to the town by Mary Queen of Scots. It is alleged she stayed briefly at Seagate Castle, which overlooks the harbour. The castle remains are protected as a Category A building and there's a plague at the castle entrance stated she stayed there in 1563.

Up until 1921 both clubs had enjoyed free Marymass Saturdays to allow the people of the town to head to the races at Irvine Moor, but in this particular year the rivals were given a league fixture against each other on that festive weekend. The decision was taken to play the match on the Friday evening instead, which proved to be a great success. The Irvine Herald reported, "Fortunately the night was ideal and there was a great crowd in Meadow Park as the teams took the field".

The Irvine derby dates back to 1905, when the first fixture took place at Victoria Park in the newly formed, but short lived Northern District League. The match was played in a gale force wind as Meadow raced into a 4-0 half time lead, however Vics hit back in the second half with the wind behind their backs to score five without reply and win the match 5-4.

I purchased my trains tickets upon my Spanish return on the previous Sunday afternoon, the late booking meant that yet again, it was via the Carlisle route, taking the same early trains as my recent trips north. Just as the train approached the outskirts of Glasgow, the bright sunshine suddenly disappeared and a grey blanket of mist descended over the city. The weather forecast was good for the afternoon, but there had been a lot of rain over the last few days, so I thought it best to check my Scottish Juniors clubs list on twitter to see if the match was in danger. The latest tweet at the top of the feed was from East Kilbride Thistle, with the news that their match was off followed by Johnstone Burgh saying their game was on. As it turned out my brief spell of postponement anxiety was a false alarm, as the East Kilbride game was the only one that didn't go ahead, so it was a huge relief I went there last month instead of today.

I caught the Irvine train just after noon, the 30-mile journey took just under half an hour so I had plenty of time to spare before the 2 o'clock kick off. The former royal burgh and new town is located on the coast of the Firth of Clyde in North Ayrshire, exactly halfway between Glasgow and Ayr, with a population of over 33,000. The town was made a Royal Burgh in 1372 by Robert II and has historical maritime connections. The harbour became a major west coast seaport and now houses the main site of the Scottish Maritime Museum.

It was the site of Scotland's 12th century Military Capital and former headquarters of the Lord High Constable of Scotland, also serving as the Capital of Cunninghame and at the time of David I, Robert II and Robert III one of the earliest capitals of Scotland. Robbie Burns knocked around Irvine in his youth, having worked in a flax mill on the Glasgow Vennel, which was a good enough reason to have a couple of streets in Irvine taking his name, with both Burns Street and Burns Crescent named in his honour.

Irvine was officially designated as a "New Town" in 1966, the fifth and last to be developed in Scotland and the only one to be located on the coast. During the writing of this book I've visited three of the five new towns in Scotland. The other two are Livingston and Cumbernauld, which I've previously "ticked" seeing "Livi" at Almondvale and Clyde FC at the Broadwood Stadium in Cumbernauld so I've accidently completed another set.

Irvine is the birthplace of the present First Minister of Scotland and SNP leader (and Jimmy Krankie lookalike) Nicola Sturgeon and Roddy Woomble, lead singer of indie rockers Idlewild. I saw the band play at Meadowbank Stadium in 2005, sandwiched in between two of my all-time favourite bands - the Pixies and Teenage Fanclub. Although I'm not a fan of the band, I did enjoy a storming set from Roddy's band on that damp windy summer's evening in Edinburgh.

My first port of call was obvious, the Rivergate Shopping Centre has a huge range of shopping outlets but I wasn't there for the retail therapy, as there's a JD Wetherspoon's, so it was lunch and a pint in The Auld Brig. There was also another pub on my must visit list alongside the harbour. The Ship Inn is the oldest public house in Irvine, which dates to 1595 and has served beer since 1754. The bar is decorated with Maritime murals and a ship mast forms part of the main bar structure and serves a selection of ale from the Ayr Brewing Company.

I should have really went to The Ship first as I had to double back on myself, leaving a canny 20-minute walk across the river to Meadow Park. When I arrived at the ground there was a noticeable police presence, just on the off chance of any local enmity getting out of hand. As I approached the turnstile I was stopped by a steward and a policeman who wanted the search my bag for weapons. I told them both not to worry as "I wasn't here to kill anyone" before adding "well … I'm not planning to anyway" Thankfully they both saw the funny side with the young constable going into fits of laughter over my throwaway remark.

Any football ground enthusiast can't help but be impressed by Meadow Park. It has a smart classic old style stand which holds 700 seats, with the social club, changing rooms and refreshment bar underneath. The ground has a capacity of 5,200 with plenty of proper terracing and in its heyday 13,740 gathered for a Junior Cup 5th Round tie with Stonehouse Violet in 1949.

Irving Meadow XI formed in 1897 and have a proud history including some unique records. The Medal have lifted the Scottish Junior Cup on three occasions, winning 2-1 against both Shettleston in 1959 and Glenafton Athletic in 1963. They completed their hat-trick ten years later finally overcoming Cambuslang Rangers 1-0 in the second replay following 2-2 and 3-3 draws. They've also finished runners-up twice, losing out to Bo'ness United in 1948, in a season when a record total of 221,500 spectators attended matches during their campaign. Meadow's 1-0 defeat to Petershill in 1951 was played in front of a record Junior Cup final crowd of 77,650 at Hampden Park.

The club issued a programme for the match and in a section titled 'Startling Statistics' it stated some unique facts about the club. For example, they were the first

Junior club to have a home game televised, when highlights of the Scottish Junior Cup tie with Fauldhouse United in 1958 was shown on Scot sport. Then on a winter Saturday in 1962 when the senior fixtures all fell foul to the weather, Scottish TV raced to Meadow Park for the big cup tie with Dundee Downfield, with the Medda turning on the style in front of the cameras, recording a 9-1 victory in which was the first Junior fixture featured as the programme's main match.

Following their 1959 success in the Junior Cup they were invited by Birmingham City to fly down to the Midlands to play a match under the floodlights at St Andrews. This was the first time a Junior club had played against English opposition, when they unlucky to lose, going down 4-3 to a last minute winning penalty.

More football first feats for the club include the first Junior club to beat a senior side in a competitive game when they beat Arbroath 1-0 in the third round of the Scottish Cup in 2009. This was followed by being the first club to face an SPL side in a competitive match, when they faced Hibernian in the next round at Easter Road, losing 3-0 in January 2010.

Since the reformation of the Junior leagues they have been SJFA West Super League Premier Division Champions, lifting the title three times in four seasons between 2009 and 2012. This follows nine Ayrshire First Division titles and an array of cup honours throughout their history, including the royal blue ribbons decorating the West of Scotland Cup nine times and the Ayrshire Cup on fourteen occasions.

Both sides went into the game without a League win this season in the Super League First Division, however they both recorded wins in the Junior Cup the previous weekend, with the likes of Hurlford United, Cumnock and Largs Thistle crashing out. As it turned out it was the Medda who claimed local bragging rights, coming from behind to claim the three points in this Irvine derby. Victoria took the lead in the 11th minute with a peach of a goal from Paul Young, who picked up the ball on the left edge of the penalty area and fired in off the far post. A good spell of pressure from the home side saw them draw level on 23 minutes, when a low hard cross from the left was turned into his own net by the defender. With their tails up they grabbed the lead before the break, when a cleared right wing corner was quickly recycled into the area to the unmarked Ryan Begley to head in at the far post.

After a good opening 45 minutes, the second half didn't quite live up to expectations. Meadow were the better side but chances were few and far between. The Wee Vics might have got something out of the game, but their cause wasn't helped by the referee who sent off Scott Chesney on 79 minutes for two yellow card offenses. Medda sealed victory with just a few minutes remaining, when a long pass found man of the match Ben Black, who beat the outcoming 'keeper to the ball to toe-poke into the net.

Afterwards I visited my usual haunts in Glasgow before heading down to Carlisle, when an enjoyable trouble free day nearly ended in calamity. I killed the three-quarters of an hour before my train home with a couple of scoops in the William Rufus pub. I was standing watching the football on TV minding my own business when suddenly a western saloon type bar brawl took place next to where I stood. I was lucky to avoid serious injury, with shards of glass flying in my direction as some knacker went ballistic with his mates, before announcing his departure by hurled a bar stool in their direction. I always profess that it's a small world and this point was proved yet again when I was rescued by a lass from Crook, who I coincidence just met on holiday in Salou last week. The happenstance of me being in a random Carlisle boozer at the same time as a newly acquainted gang of women from deepest County Durham is quite astounding.

So, that's the penultimate club in this project which has took over my life over the last two seasons. I'm keeping everything crossed that Arthurlie have a home fixture on my next planned trip to Glasgow at the end of this month. This will be my last visit north in 2016 as I've got prior engagements for my time off in November and as far as the winter months are concerned it's a "no" from me. My aim right at the start of the book was to complete the set by the end of the year, so as things stand there's a fifty-fifty chance I'll complete this challenge in a few weeks' time, to finally finish my trail of the Scottish Holy Grail.

Matchday Stats

Saturday 1st October 2016 (2pm ko)

West Region Super League First Division

Irvine Meadow XI 3(OG 23 Begley 38 Black 87)

Irvine Victoria FC 1(Young 11)

Att.400est

Ground no.549

28. Well That Was Easy

Arthurlie - Underlie Park (October 2016)

There's a wise old saying in my part of the world which proclaims "shy bairns get nowt!" After the Irvine trip I was tempted to contact the West Region SJFA to gently nudge them into fixing one fixtures in my favour. Just a simple request to have Arthurlie playing at home on the 27th October. I decided in the end to let fate take its natural course as the uncertainty and apprehension is all part of the fun. In the meantime, the next round of the Junior Cup was made, with Arthurlie giving an away tie at Kilwinning Rangers on the 20th of October, which meant if that game was a draw then the replay would be the following Saturday, which nicely ties in with my trip.

As it happens James Little contacted me on Wednesday the 19th, to let me know the fixtures were out and Arthurlie were at home in either the cup replay or a league fixture against Hurlford United. I was obviously delighted with this fantastic news, as the trail of the Holy Grail would be completed and the "From the Toon to the Scottish Joons Finale Party" was good to go!

Arthurlie FC has turned out to be the book's very own Shangri-La. The 'Lie were set to be the first ground I visited when I started out on this quest in January last year, but they were one of many games that fell foul to the weather on that afternoon. Another postponement occurred again in late November, followed by the

Whitburn debacle at the start of this year, when a trip to Barrhead was lined up in the backup plan. After three failed attempts, it's little wonder that Arthurlie appears as the final chapter in this story.

The finale party wasn't as popular has I had initially planned it. Unfortunately, my good pal "Jimmy Jimmy" couldn't make it due to work commitments, followed by the bitter blow of not having Plymouth Pete with us, as a family bereavement the previous evening meant he obviously had to drop out. Honest Paul was making his third appearance in this tale and more importantly on this occasion, so was my bessie mate Zippy, as this was also his birthday beano.

Zippy, also known by his old schoolmates as "Flop" or more formally Darren (as his mother calls him) has been a great friend of mine since we first met when working together in 1987. We obviously have a lot in common, sharing a passion for football, betting, Horse Racing and obviously, a good session on the lash. The main thing that brought us together apart from both supporting NUFC is our love of good guitar based music. When we both worked at Traidcraft on the Team Valley he got me heavily into The Smiths and Big Country, while I drew his ears to likes of The Cure and the Wedding Present. When the temporary job at the factory ended, we kept in touch with each other becoming bosom buddies, later becoming my best man at my wedding and Godfather to my son James.

Also, joining us for the final match was James Little, who as I predicted at the start of the book, has played a crucial part in successfully and swiftly visiting these Junior Cup winners. We met up with James at Haymarket station to catch our connection to Glasgow Queen Street, where we arrived at 11.40.

As this was Zippy's birthday there had to be a decent pub crawl lined up. We started off with breakfast and a bevvy in the Camperdown Place, where over our sausages and eggs discussed which actors would play us if this book was made into a film. My part would be played by Tony Danza, the former TV star of American series *Taxi* and *Who's the Boss?* Although thinking about it now, in my teenage years a lad called Burnsy used to call me Omar after the film star Omar Sharif. I thought he was taking the piss until I discovered who he was, being a Hollywood heartthrob and a big hit with the ladies.

As for the rest of the cast James would be played by Radio 2 DJ Ken Bruce as he has the accent and the baldy knappa. Paul would be played by Morrissey, however when we went to Liverpool in the summer, a bloke on the train said he looks the spitting dabs of actor Michael Elphick. Darren was a tough one, in the 80's he looked like singer Paul Young, then in the 90's resembled former Chelsea, Southampton and Crystal Palace striker Neil Shipperley, although thankfully he doesn't look like him now. (check out Shipperley on Google images to find out why)

After devouring our blotting paper our boozer crawl continued at the Counting House, The Auctioneer and The Royal Scot, before we caught the 1342 train for the ten-minute journey to Barrhead. The town is on the edge of the Gleniffer Braes, eight miles south-west of the city centre. Barrhead formed when the neighbouring villages of Arthurlie, Grahamston and Gateside gradually merged to form one contiguous town. The name "Barrhead" first appeared in 1750, deriving from the agricultural term Barr meaning long ploughed furrows of crops, as the original homestead lay at the head of the barrs.

The town was a major centre for manufacturing during the 19th and early 20th century in iron foundry, tannery and porcelain ware works, until the decline and closure of nearly all these industries at the end of the last century. Nowadays Barrhead is a popular residential commuter town for nearby Paisley and Glasgow, in a part of the world which according to *Reader's Digest* magazine is the second-best place in the UK to raise a family.

On arrival, we called into the Brig Inn opposite the rail station, which made a refreshing change to some of the local pubs I've experienced in some parts of Scotland. The pub was full of football memorabilia covering all clubs, with an equal array of photographs and programmes from Celtic and Rangers. The walls were also decorated with Scottish international programmes and other football clubs from both sides of the border, making it a sort of Swiss type neutral drinking zone, where everyone is welcome.

When we got to Dunterlie Park, Darren took a picture of me outside the turnstile entrance celebrating reaching my Shangri-La. The picture shows my elation in finishing my list and the old codgers in queue chuckling away, wondering what the big deal is. Arthurlie have played at a few grounds named Dunterlie Park and have resided at the current one since 1919. The entrance is at the top of the terrace behind the goal, with the terracing continuing to the west side of the ground where there's an enclosure, decked out in club colours with the club name on the front of the roof. The rest of the 4,000-capacity ground is open with a dugout on each side, with the changing rooms and the 1874 Club cabin behind the far goal.

The football club was founded in 1874, being one of five surviving teams that played in the Scottish Cup in their formative season, later becoming one of the founder members of the Scottish Federation League in 1892. The club played at senior level until 1929, within the Scottish Football League between 1901 and 1915, then after the First World War in the newly created Third Division in 1923. Arthurlie were Third Division championship in their debut season, followed by four reasonably successful campaigns in the Second Division until financial problems forced the club to resign during the 1928–29 season.

The club joined the Junior ranks in 1931, winning the Scottish Junior Cup for the first time in 1937 with an emphatic 5–1 win over Kirkintilloch Rob Roy in the final. They were runners-up to Fauldhouse in 1946, then over sixty years since their first success finally lifted the famous trophy again. In 1998 they faced their near rivals Pollok at Fir Park, recording a fabulous 4–0 victory, gaining sweet revenge after losing 1-0 to their adversaries in the 1981 final. The scorers that afternoon were Mark McLaughlin, Steven Convery, Steven Nugent and John Millar who managed Beith Juniors to Junior Cup success last season.

"The 'Lie" have gathered a collection of cup honours over their distinguished history, including the West Scotland Challenge Cup on five occasions. They won the Central League Premier Division four times, the last of which was the season before the reconstruction of the West Region in 2001. The club were placed in the Superleague First Division, becoming champions in 2002-03, and since winning promotion to the West Superleague Premier

Division they have been pipped to the league title as runners-up four times. The trophy cabinet has also been stocked with seven League Cup's and the Sectional League Cup four times, the last of which came in 2010.

The Junior Cup 2nd Round clash the previous Saturday finished goalless, so I was thrilled with a big cup tie to finish off with. As Kilwinning Rangers were the opponents this rounded the story off nicely, as they were also the away team in my very first Junior match, plus my visit to Abbey Park coincided with the week of my 50th birthday. The Buffs booked their place in the 3rd round with an impressive away performance. The took the lead on 13 minutes when the home defence failed to deal with a corner kick. Gavin Hay made a good save from the initial header, but Iain Cashmore was on hand to net the rebound from close range. The visitors could have extended their lead but the Lie got back into it just before half time, when a free kick from the right was met with a free header from Ryan McGregor.

Arthurlie sporting their Argentine style sky blue and white striped shirts hit the woodwork twice before the Buffs regained the advantage on 64 minutes with a superb strike from Ben Lewis, who latched onto a through ball and curled his shot high inside the 'keeper's left hand post. With just a few minutes left Kilwinning wrapped it up when Frye laid the ball into the path of Liam McGuiness for an easy finish before celebrating with the visiting supporters behind the goal.

Just before the end of the game James introduced me to Neil Edgar, who is a regular contributor to the 100 grounds club Facebook page. He posts some cracking pictures of the matches he attends around Scotland, so it was good to finally meet him. He just happened to mention that there should be a steward's inquiry into this match, because when he attends a Junior game there's always a sending off. Within a minute of his remark a disappointing afternoon for Arthurlie was summed up in stoppage time when a late lunge from Jordan Leyden resulted in a straight red card. My birthday present to my pal Zippy of introducing him to Junior football went down well, as it was an enjoyable game and a typical all action Scottish Cup tie.

After the game, we called at The Horseshoe Bar, the Drum & Monkey and The Maltman in Glasgow, before saying our farewells to James, as we boarded the 1840 train to Carlisle. We were expecting to have an hour and a half in Carlisle, but ended up getting the 1938 instead of the 2124 train back home. This service was half an hour late because the train needed to be expanded due to a large following of Toon fans coming back from Preston. The change to the train schedule meant we were home quicker, allowing time for a few pints on home soil, instead of risking the western bar brawl sort of incident that happened on my last visit to the border town.

At the end of the night there was just me and the birthday boy left drinking in the Bridge Hotel. We reflected on a cracking day and the end of my personal journey, which has been easier and more enjoyable than I imagined. To be honest I was on a bit of a downer the following week, as it began to dawn on me that my latest obsession in completing another list was all crossed off, with no pending excursions north to look forward to.

During the writing of this book many people have asked why I chose Scotland as its subject matter. The simple reason is, I've always got on well with the Scots and never had a crossed word with anyone north of Berwick. Maybe that's because the people of the north-east have a similar nature, always willing to socialise, be cordial or help a stranger in need. There's an old saying that Scotsmen are just Geordies with their brains smashed in. Come to think of it maybe I got that myth the wrong way around, but what do I know? I'm just a thick Geordie!

I plan to take some time out before embarking on my new Groundhopping challenge, which at the moment I have absolutely no idea what that may be. Although come to think of it, there is another 22 existing winners of the Junior Cup who lifted the trophy before I was born, so maybe there is sequel on the cards, embarking on another quest from the Toon to the Joons on the trail of the Scottish Holy Grail.

Matchday Stats

Saturday 29th October 2016 (2.30pm ko)

Scottish Junior Cup Round 2 replay Replay

Arthurlie 1(McGregor 39)

Kilwinning Rangers 3(Cashmore 13 Lewis 64 McGuiness 88)

Att.500est

Ground no.551

Pictures from the grounds and matches featured in this book can be viewed on my website;

100groundsclub.blogspot.co.uk

Follow on Twitter;

@ShauneeBoy100FgC

Check out my Groundhopping Facebook page;

www.facebook.com/groups/100FgC

From the Toon to the Joons

The Album

Thank you for reading my book. I hope you enjoyed it. If you weren't too fussed on it then may I offer you this soundtrack as a way of compensation.

You probably worked out that each chapter was named after a song, but extra bonus points if you worked out that every track was performed by a Scottish band.

You can listen to the complete album at your leisure on YouTube by copying this link;

From the Toon to the Joons - The Album: http://www.youtube.com/playlist?list=PLFoZ V8idV6vQ3leWI-MgexMlm_2vymvL9

1. The Concept - Teenage Fanclub

(released as a single from the 1991 album Bandwagonesque)

2. High Tide Low Tide - The Vaselines

(available on the 2014 album V for Vaselines)

3. Out of Town - The Skids

(available on the 1980 album The Absolute Game)

4. Everything's Roses - The Fire Engines

(released as a single in 1980 and available on the compilation album Codex Teenage Premonition)

5. Let's Make Some Plans - Close Lobsters

(released as a single in 1987 and available on Forever! Until Victory)

6. Steeltown - Big Country

(taking from the 1985 album Steeltown)

7. A Heady Tale - The Fratellis

(from the 2006 album Costello Music)

8.Blue Soap - The Associates

(B side of the 1981 single 'Message Oblique Speech' available on the CD Fourth Drawer Down)

9.Top of the Pops - The Rezillos

(released as a single in 1978 and taking from the album Can't Stand The Rezillos)

10. Satellite City - Orange Juice

(available on the 1982 album You Can't Hide Love Forever)

11. Life is a Motorway - The Supernaturals

(available on the 2002 album What We Did Last Summer)

12. Blue Desire - The Silencers

(From the 1987 album, A Letter from St. Paul)

13. Happy Birthday - Altered Images

(Released as a single in 1981 from the same titled album)

14. Saturday Superhouse - Biffy Clyro

(Released as a single in 2007 from the album Puzzle)

15. The Drinking Eye - Arab Strap

(From the 1999 album Elephant Shoe)

16. Maybe I Should Drive - Trash Can Sinatras

(From the 1990 album Cake)

17. Hey Mr Smith - Fingerprintz

(From the 1979 album The Very Dab)

18. Road, River and Rail - Cocteau Twins

(from the 1990 album Heaven or Las Vegas)

19. Live In A Hiding Place - Idlewild

(From the 2002 album, The Remote Part)

20. The Hard One - The Beta Band

(From the 1999 album, The Beta Band)

21. Glittering Prize - Simple Minds

(Hit single in 1982 from the album New Gold Dream)

22. Goodwill City - Goodbye Mr Mackenzie

(From the 1989 album, Good Deeds and Dirty Rags)

23. Black and White Unite - Belle & Sebastian

(From the 2002 album Storytelling)

24. King of the Castle - Soup Dragons

(From the 1988 album, This Is Our Art)

25. Why Does It Always Rain on Me? - Travis

(Hit single from the 1999 album The Man Who)

26. Head On - Jesus & Mary Chain

(From the 1989 album, Automatic)

27. Let Mother Nature Be Your Guide - BMX Bandits

(From the 1990 album C86)

28. Well That Was Easy - Franz Ferdinand

(from the 2005 album, You Could Have It So Much Better)

Lifetime Cup Winners

1965/66 Bonnyrigg Rose 6 Whitburn 1 (after a 1-1 draw)

1966/67 Kilsyth Rangers 3 Rutherglen Glencairn 1 (after a 1-1 draw)

1967/68 Johnstone Burgh 4 Glenrothes 3 (after a 2-2 draw)

1968/69 Cambuslang Rangers 1 Kirkintilloch Rob Roy 0

1969/70 Blantyre Vics 1 Penicuik Athletic 0 (after a 1-1 draw)

1970/71 Cambuslang Rangers 2 Newtongrange Star 1

1971/72 Cambuslang Rangers 3 Bonnyrigg Rose 2 (after a 1-1 draw)

1972/73 Irvine Meadow 1 Cambuslang Rangers 0 (after 3-3 and 2-2 draws)

1973/74 Cambuslang Rangers 3 Linlithgow Rose 1

1974/75 Glenrothes 1 Rutherglen Glencairn 0

1975/76 Bo`ness United 3 Darvel 0

1976/77 Kilbirnie Ladeside 3 Kirkintilloch Rob Roy 1

1977/78 Bonnyrigg Rose 1 Stonehouse Violet 0

1978/79 Cumnock 1 Bo'ness United 0

1979/80 Baillieston 2 Benburb 0 (A.E.T.) (after a 2-2 draw)

1980/81 Pollok 1 Arthurlie 0

1981/82 Blantyre Victoria 1 Baillieston 0

1982/83 East Kilbride Thistle 2 Bo'ness United 0

1983/84 Bo`ness United 2 Baillieston 0

1984/85 Pollok 3 Petershill 1 (after a 1-1 draw)

1985/86 Auchinleck Talbot 3 Pollok 2

1986/87 Auchinleck Talbot 1 Kilbirnie Ladeside 0 (after a 1-1 draw)

1987/88 Auchinleck Talbot 1 Petershill 0

1988/89 Cumnock Juniors 1 Ormiston Primrose 0

1989/90 Hill of Beath Hawthorn 1 Lesmahagow 0

1990/91 Auchinleck Talbot 1 Newtongrange Star 0

1991/92 Auchinleck Talbot 4 Glenafton 0

1992/93 Glenafton 1 Tayport 0

1993/94 Largs Thistle 1 Glenafton 0

1994/95 Camelon 2 Whitburn 0

1995/96 Tayport 2 Camelon 0 (A.E.T.)

 1996/97 Pollok 3 Tayport 1

1997/98 Arthurlie 4 Pollok 0

1998/99 Kilwinning Rangers 1 Kelty Hearts 0

1999/00 Whitburn 2 Johnstone Burgh 2 (A.E.T.) (Whitburn won 4-3 on penalties)

2000/01 Renfrew 0 Carnoustie Panmure 0 (A.E.T.) (Renfrew won 6-5 on penalties)

2001/02 Linlithgow Rose 1 Auchinleck Talbot 0

2002/03 Tayport 1 Linlithgow Rose 0

2003/04 Carnoustie Panmure 0 Tayport 0 (A.E.T.) (Carnoustie won 5-4 on penalties)

2004/05 Tayport 2 Lochee United 0

2005/06 Auchinleck Talbot 2 Bathgate Thistle 1

2006/07 Linlithgow Rose 2 Kelty Hearts 1

2007/08 Bathgate Thistle 2 Cumnock Juniors 1

2008/09 Auchinleck Talbot 2 Clydebank 1

2009/10 Linlithgow Rose 1 Largs Thistle 0

2010/11 Auchinleck Thistle 2 Musselburgh 1

2011/12 Shotts Bon Accord 2 Auchinleck Talbot 1

2012/13 Auchinleck Talbot 1 Linlithgow Rose 0

2013/14 Hurlford United 3 Glenafton Athletic 0

2014/15 Auchinleck Talbot 2 Musselburgh 1

2015/16 Beith Juniors 1 Pollok 1 (Beith won 4-3 on penalties)

Acknowledgments

To my darling wife, Debra for over twenty years of love, peace, harmony and understanding. x

To Laura and James for accepting their Dad's obsessions and eccentricities as they were growing up. xx

Love to my Mam and sister Gillian. I hope you now understand why I was away from home a lot. xx

A huge thank you to James Little for being my travel companion, chauffeur, drinking buddy and co-star in this story.

To Lee Stewart, Katie Wallace, Jamie McQueen, Darren Turnbull, Paul Gray, Mark Wilkins, Donald McCrorie, David Stoker, Joris Van de Wier, Harry Watson, Ivan Hay, Chris Sanderson, Anders Johansen, Graham and Lois Crofts for playing their parts in this journey.

Special thanks to Steven Charlton, Stephen Dobson, Alan Oliver, James Morton, Peter Harding, Jonathan Elton, Dan Gooch, Mark Thompson and Graham Precious for their support and words of encouragement throughout the years.

Last but by no means least, all the very best to the clubs featured in this book for their warmth and hospitality. You are a credit to football, the SJFA and the Scottish nation.

About the Author

Shaun was born in the mid sixties on the very same night that Bob Dylan controversially plugged in a guitar for the first time live at the Newport folk festival.

His birthplace was a mile away from St James Park and just along the road from Gateshead's old Redheugh Park ground, so he was born to be football daft and a stadium enthusiast.

He attended his first Newcastle United match as an 8-year-old in 1974 and learned quickly that football is an emotional rollercoaster, in floods of tears as the Magpies were hammered by Liverpool in the FA Cup final.

He also follows his hometown club Gateshead, seeing his first game at the International Stadium in 1978, before becoming a more regular supporter in 2004 when the club almost went out of business.

He left school in 1981 with no prospects because of high unemployment under Thatcher's Tory government. After being in and out of work he finally got himself a "proper job" in 1988, joining Royal Mail as a postman, delivering letters and parcels in his hometown now for almost 30 years.

His other main interest is music, being a keen record collector, gig goer and a dodgy bass guitarist. His love of great bands span the decades from The Beatles to punk, ska to indie, shoegazing to power pop!

In July 2006, he formed - The 100 Football Grounds Club and began writing an award-winning blog about his travels. This was the first website for supporters to log their football grounds, with the blog accumulated reports and pictures from over 500 matches throughout the years.

Shaun finally settled down and became a family man in 1995. Punching above his weight by marrying the delectable Debra and together they produced two wonderful children, Laura and James.

12757403R00115

Printed in Great Britain
by Amazon